The Masculinity Conspiracy

JOSEPH GELFER

Published by Joseph Gelfer via CreateSpace | www.gelfer.net

Cover image: the author in Albion by Laki Sideris

ISBN-13: 978-1463781705

ISBN-10: 1463781709

ABOUT THE BOOK

This is a reformatted edition of the free online book *The Masculinity Conspiracy*. The text of the online version may change over time relative to this edition. Feel free to come along and join the discussion around the book at:
http://masculinityconspiracy.com

Some parts of this book are extracted from the following previous publications by the author: *Numen, Old Men: Contemporary Masculine Spiritualities and the Problem of Patriarchy* (Equinox Publishing, 2009); "Review of 'No More Christian Nice Guy' by Paul Coughlin." *The Journal of Men's Studies* 14, no. 2 (2006): 259-60; "Review of 'The Hidden Spirituality of Men: Ten Metaphors to Awaken the Sacred Masculine' by Matthew Fox." *Journal of Men, Masculinities and Spirituality* 3, no. 1 (2009): 94-96; various blog posts at: **http://www.gelfer.net**.

CONTENTS

1: CONSPIRACY, PROBLEM, SOLUTION

The Conspiracy

I want to start with an exercise, one that is going to put a slightly different spin on reality. It's a very small investment of effort and time. There's no need here to meditate in an Indian ashram, or guzzle some psychedelic brew in the Amazonian rainforest. It takes five minutes, and you can do it at home for free. We're going to look through the looking glass, quite literally.

Go and find a mirror. Look at yourself in the mirror closely for a full five minutes. Look first into your eyes, notice their color and pattern. See the imperfections in your skin, the asymmetry to some parts of your face. Twitch your nose, and have a think about how that thought signal reaches your nose, and that your intention to twitch seems almost unrelated to the act itself. Contemplate the idea that it is the person in the mirror who moves through the world and that everyone sees and interacts with, not you. Notice that there is an increasingly large disconnect between who you feel you are and the person in the mirror, a distance between the two yous that is difficult to articulate in words. Now imagine that gap between the mirror and every man in the world alive right now. That's a lot of gaps, right? Now imagine that gap for every man who has ever lived. That's a lot of disconnect, a vast space between men and the men in the mirror. This is the space we're going to navigate in this book. It's in this space of disconnect that we can locate the Masculinity Conspiracy. But what exactly is the Masculinity Conspiracy? A brief definition of terms is in order.

For starters, what is masculinity? Getting into this is rather premature, as the manipulation of its meaning is at the very heart of the conspiracy. Nevertheless, some immediate definition is required to progress. To begin with, masculinity is *not* what "men do": this is a very common misconception that causes all sorts of trouble. To get to the meaning of this, it's useful first to explore the sex/gender distinction. Sex and gender are routinely used interchangeably. For example, I often see a section on administrative forms called "gender" in which I am asked to tick the "male" or "female" box. Here's the difference between the two, largely accepted by researchers of sex and gender: sex is biological, gender is socially constructed.

The concept that sex is biological is easy enough to grasp. We are generally born either male or female (even if the percentage of people born with ambiguous sexual organs— hermaphrodites, now more accurately referred to as intersex—is surprisingly high). Again, biological sex is "male" and "female." When those administrative forms ask us to tick male or female, that section should more accurately be called "sex," not "gender." But, gender is socially constructed? This requires some more careful thinking.

Gender is a spectrum of codes that can be applied to and describe men's and women's behaviors. Gender is "masculine" and "feminine." There are two important things to remember about gender. First, that which is recognized as gender (in our case, masculinity) changes in space and time. For example, in Detroit it is not the done thing for two men to hold hands in the street unless they want to be considered gay. The gender code of the space of Detroit says masculinity is not about holding hands.

However, if you hopped on a plane to Delhi, you would see men holding hands all over the place without any assumption of them being gay. The gender code of the space of Delhi says masculinity *is* about holding hands. That's space, but what about time? Think about fashion. Today, back on the streets of Detroit (sorry, Detroit: you don't deserve to be singled out like this), it is not the done thing for men to wear frilly shirts unless they want to be considered effeminate thespians. The gender code of today's time in Detroit says masculinity is not about frilly shirts. However, if you hopped in a time machine to Tudor England, you would see very manly men wearing frilly shirts all over the place. The gender code of the time of Tudor England says masculinity *is* about frilly shirts. So, what we mean by "masculinity" shifts constantly depending on *where* and *when* we are.

The second thing to remember about gender is that it is not as obviously connected to sex as you might imagine. The feminist philosopher Judith Butler makes an excellent case for this in her book *Gender Trouble: Feminism and the Subversion of Identity*. The common assumption is that masculinity (even its differing forms in space and time) is something done by men, whereas femininity is something done by women. Often this is true, but it doesn't have to be. Men can be feminine, and women masculine. The obvious (and rather blunt) example is feminine gay men and masculine gay women. However, it applies in all situations, to all people: all men have feminine aspects, all women have masculine aspects. Sometimes these are very subtle; sometimes they are so extreme you might have a hard time telling if someone is a man or a woman. And all of this is perfectly normal.

In short, masculinity is a vast spectrum of differing gender performances. Indeed, to use the term "masculinity" in the singular is rather misleading: it should really be "masculinit*ies*," in the plural. And masculinity can apply just as easily to women as it does to men. Now that we see how much more complex gender is compared to sex, it becomes easier to imagine that there is plenty going on that might be feeding into the Masculinity Conspiracy. So let's look now at what "conspiracy" means.

The popular definition of conspiracy can be found in the idea of a cover-up, and to a large degree this is certainly the case. However, there are various aspects to conspiracy that are worth unpacking. In his book, *A Culture of Conspiracy: Apocalyptic Visions in Contemporary America*, political scientist Michael Barkun claims conspiracy is a method through which people explain the presence of evil in the world. They do this by viewing "history as controlled by massive, demonic forces." Conspiracies can therefore be seen as simultaneously frightening and reassuring: the demonic forces are at work, but at least they can be identified as the source of everything around us that is bad, as opposed to the true terror of random evil.

Barkun identifies three key aspects to conspiracy theories, which are worth spelling out. First, *nothing happens by accident*: there is always intent behind actions; the willed nature of reality is paramount. Second, *nothing is as it seems*: the source of a conspiracy tends to conceal its activities through the appearance of innocence or misinformation. Third, *everything is connected*: patterns abound in conspiracy; exposing conspiracy is about unveiling these hidden connections. Barkun sees this type of thinking (which has escalated since 9/11) as ultimately resulting in paranoia: a closed system of ideas that "defeat any attempt at testing" due to the assumption that all the evidence countering the conspiracy must be *part* of the conspiracy, and therefore rejected.

To be fair, Barkun is highly critical of conspiracy belief, and when you look at the examples he provides such as the Illuminati and extraterrestrial reptilian masters, it is tempting to agree with him. But because conspiracy theories can often be a bit flaky (who can resist the description "Barkun mad"?), it doesn't mean that they are *always* flaky, or that at the very least there aren't some reasonable things that *resemble* conspiracies, inasmuch as

4

there being a widespread assumption that needs to be exposed as false.

And this is what I'm getting at with the Masculinity Conspiracy. In this book I will argue that the way masculinity has been sold to us has *the appearance* of a conspiracy. Looking at the proceeding evidence, it appears that the way we define masculinity has not happened by accident. It appears that nothing about masculinity is as it commonly seems. It appears that a number of key themes in society are connected to form a legitimizing framework for the Masculinity Conspiracy. What I'm *not* suggesting is that the Masculinity Conspiracy is "controlled by massive, demonic forces." I use the term "conspiracy" fully aware of its limitations, and somewhat tongue-in-cheek. Besides, if I had called this book *The Masculinity Phenomenon that Shares Some Loose Commonality with Barkun's Presentation of Conspiracy Belief*, you just wouldn't have read it, would you?

So, now that we have some definition of terms on the table, we can get down to introducing the business at hand. The Masculinity Conspiracy plays out in diverse ways. In fact, there are not many aspects of our experience that escape its influence. In this book I'm only going to scratch the surface by addressing some broad themes where the Masculinity Conspiracy is at its most potent. But remember, this is just a jumping off point: the chapters are grouped around high-level themes, but the conspiracy runs deep. Specifically, the book is grouped around chapters addressing History, Sexuality, Relationships, Fatherhood, Archetypes, and Spirituality. The following paragraphs give a snapshot of these themes: these are the primary elements of the Masculinity Conspiracy that will be exposed as *confining* rather than *defining* masculinity.

History. The Masculinity Conspiracy appeals to history in two fundamental ways. The first argument focuses on biological determinism, which means that men are physically programmed in a certain way, which both explains and justifies certain male behaviors. The second argument focuses on the social construction of history, which means that because men have historically done things in a certain way that has been largely accepted by society, they should continue to do so today.

Sexuality. The Masculinity Conspiracy frames sexuality in two fundamental ways. First, following biological determinism, it is suggested that men are subject to certain sexual impulses, which both explain and justify male behaviors. Second, a particular form of heterosexuality is presented which suggests a natural order to the way men engage with women and with other men.

Relationships. The Masculinity Conspiracy uses its understanding of biological determinism and sexuality to frame relationships in two fundamental ways. First, relations between men and women echo the age-old roles of hunter, nurturer and so on, which largely allocate men and women to the public and private domains respectively. Second, relations between all people are ordered in a way for men to achieve success in the eyes of both men and women.

Fatherhood. The Masculinity Conspiracy distills the lessons learned from history, sexuality and relationships in the role of fatherhood in two fundamental ways. First, more than any other, fatherhood provides a forum through which men can understand their role in the perpetuation of the species. Second, more than any other, fatherhood provides a way of communicating the values of the Masculinity Conspiracy to the next generation.

Archetypes. The Masculinity Conspiracy interprets and uses archetypes in two fundamental ways. First, following a similar argument to biological determinism, it is suggested that archetypes are unavoidable aspects of humanity, whether hardwired in the reptilian part of our brains, or somewhere deep and undefined in our psyches. Second, following Carl Jung, it is suggested that archetypes are not just part of our psyches, but our collective unconscious which binds humanity in both space and time.

Spirituality. The Masculinity Conspiracy adopts spirituality in two fundamental ways. First, it develops the theme of archetypes, suggesting there is a spiritual realm that contains archetypal models of being a man. Second, via both the holy books of major religions and the more diverse teachings of newer faith traditions, spirituality argues that there are certain codes attributable either to enlightened human beings or some creative entity that define masculinity: these must be adhered to or we risk being out of line with the divine plan for men.

In the concluding chapter, I will draw together the lines of argument presented in the above themes. However, these themes are simply the way the Masculinity Conspiracy plays out: they do not explain *why* it plays it. In the conclusion we'll revisit that space between men and the men in the mirror, as it is in this space of disconnect that the bottom-line answers are to be found about the source of the conspiracy and all our roles within it. In short, it's about looking into those big existential issues (remember those?): freedom, isolation, meaninglessness and, ultimately, death (eek!).

The Problem

Now, you might look at those themes I've outlined above—from history through to nature—and think, *hang on a minute...* Rest assured, I will be unpacking these themes with suitable granularity. Each chapter will start just like this one started, with a section called *The Conspiracy*. These sections will outline the popular understanding of the theme at hand via one or two books that perpetuate the Masculinity Conspiracy. These books are not chosen because they play some special role in the conspiracy, rather because they provide useful examples: any number of other examples could have been selected.

These sections are about presenting the conspiracy on its own terms: a *fair go*, as we say in Australia, before I start identifying problems. This critiquing process will happen in the second section of each chapter—just like this one—called *The*

Problem. The goal of these sections is twofold: first, to identify problems in the conspiracy specifically to do with masculinity; second, to promote the kind of critical thinking required to identify and mitigate these problems.

We'll get into specific examples of this in the following chapters, but the fundamental thing to be mindful of when reading is that when popular presentations of masculinity are offered in *The Conspiracy* sections a suggestion is made (to put it mildly) about the *appropriateness* of these issues for men. This is often achieved by putting a qualifying word in front of "masculinity." For example, various forms of Christian men's movement might speak in terms of "biblical masculinity." The use of "biblical" here is intended to communicate that this is not some new-fangled masculinity—the like of which has resulted in today's "crisis of masculinity"—rather, "proper" masculinity. Now let's say, for argument's sake, that you're no great fan of Christianity, much less using Old Testament patriarchs as a role model for contemporary men. You might, with some justification, ask, "Why should I accept biblical masculinity as a model for men? What possible relevance can this have for me?" I hope you *would* ask these questions, *particularly* if you were a Christian.

But there's something else going on here. The use of the term "biblical" not only suggests a "proper" masculinity, but also some kind of bottom line that cannot be further reduced or questioned. In short, it is a statement of authority. Again, if you're no great fan of Christianity, this will come as no surprise to you, and may confirm your assumptions about Christianity and authority.

However (and it's a BIG however), there are various other words that perform the same function here as "biblical" that may be slipping under your radar. If you have concerns about "biblical masculinity," you should also have concerns about "real masculinity," "genuine masculinity," "authentic masculinity," "archetypal masculinity," and so on. These types of words are very common in discussions about masculinity in conservative and progressive contexts alike. But make no mistake: whenever you read such words, two things are happening. First, you are being told what masculinity *should* be about. Second, you are being told not to question why this is the case. Sometimes the people communicating these two messages are perfectly aware of what they are doing, other times they are not. In both cases we are witnessing the Masculinity Conspiracy at work. If you stop reading this book right now, here's the takeaway:

- never accept being told what masculinity *should* be about

- always question *why* you are being told what masculinity *should* be about.

This point is a useful bridge to that second goal of *The Problem* sections: critical thinking. You may remember that towards the end of the movie *The Wizard of Oz*, when the "Wizard" is exposed from behind the curtain as a mere man he shouts, "pay no attention to that man behind the curtain!" Well, I'm suggesting you pull back the curtain and pay attention to the man behind it. Expose the machinations of everything around you.

Note, for example, the familiarity you'll start to feel with the structure of this book's chapters (*The Conspiracy, The Problem, The Solution*), with the rhythm of the sentences. Everything is there for a reason: a gentle repetition that suggests a subtle feeling of order and plausibility. Now think about why I'm telling you this, exposing my authorial intention to lull you into a receptive mood. Is it for the sake of transparency, or does it serve some deeper cause? Perhaps it's the old magician's trick of misdirection? By chipping away at the different levels of meaning behind everything around us, we can slowly expose the conspiracy for what it is. In fancy terms, it's called a "hermeneutic of suspicion." A hermeneutic is a way-of-understanding-lens through which to view stuff when figuring it out. In short, assume you're being bullshitted in some way. Ask *how*. More importantly, ask *why*. Nine times out of ten you'll realize you *are* being bullshitted. On the tenth time, you might find a gem, just like this book :)

There's another thing we need to get out of the way before we start. Because I am very critical of a lot of things to do with masculinity, some people jump to the conclusion that I am anti-masculinity, or even anti-men. I have been called a man-hater, mangina, pussy-whipped, femi-Nazi, queer and all manner of other things by folks who believe I'm out to diss regular men. However, if you remember the sex/gender distinction, even if I were anti-masculinity, this is not the same thing as being anti-men, as masculinity is a gender performance that shifts in space and time, whereas men are biological realities.

But the thing is, I like men. Some of my best friends are men. I'm a male myself, as are my two sons: I like us. There's a reasonable probability that my daughter will one day marry a male: I hope to like him too. This book is not anti-men, it is anti-*a certain way* of defining masculinity. It is anti-*a certain way* of being a man that has been playing out since the dawn of humanity. Let's say it again from the other direction: this book is pro-man because it is pro-people, but in order to be pro-people we have to stop problematic ways of doing masculinity. (Of course, there are problematic ways of being feminine too, but masculinity happens to have a bigger footprint on the world. But you're most welcome to write *The Femininity Conspiracy* when you have a free moment.)

The Solution

In the past I thought that exposing and deconstructing what was wrong with something was a significant part of constructing an alternative to the subject of my critique. In particular, in my first book, *Numen, Old Men: Contemporary Masculinities and the Problem of Patriarchy* I devoted a lot of words to critiquing various forms of masculine spirituality. I released the book into the world with the assumption that these (in my mind) watertight arguments would make people cast the subjects of my critique to one side. *Quelle surprise*, I was wrong.

I received lots of feedback suggesting that while pointing out what is wrong with something piques folks' interest, it also leaves them rather cold. People don't just want to be shown what's *wrong*, they want to be shown what's *right*. Largely, I feel this has something to do with the strange relationship lots of folks seem to have with the idea of "criticism." We often hear the phrase "everyone's a critic," and this has negative connotations. In some circles, being critical is perceived as an attitude problem, or even some kind of psychological disorder that explains everything bad in one's life from a lack of satisfaction, through to illness and not being sufficiently wealthy. In this way, everyone has to be a "positive thinker" if they want to succeed in life. Barbara Ehrenreich's book *Bright-sided: How the Relentless Promotion of Positive Thinking Has Undermined America* makes a good case for how this type of thinking has become problematically engrained in society.

I certainly believe in the power of positive thinking: there is indeed a long way we can go in life on our attitude alone. However, the downside is that by shying away from criticism, our bullshit detectors are rendered silent and we remain exposed to nonsense. However, somewhat ironically, unless it is used as a way of putting people down, criticism is actually a *positive* thing: a continual process of unpacking, refinement and improvement on ideas (akin to the "scientific method"). How could it be anything other than positive? In a sense, by resisting criticism, the positive thinking crowd negates its own worldview, which ultimately leaves it in a meaningless void, or alternatively exposes its worldview as something other than positive thinking (such as a strategy to secure capital and power). But that's getting a bit critical, and is more appropriate for *The Problem* sections...

The point here is that *The Solution* sections do exactly what it says on the tin: in other words, they provide solutions. This moves beyond the mere exposing of the Masculinity Conspiracy, which is an important task, but not an end in itself. Sometimes this is going to involve looking at the same issues outlined in *The Problem* sections, but from the other—positive—direction. Sometimes this is going to involve something new about the chapter theme in question, akin to a manifesto (or if, like me, you have a weakness for puns, a MANifesto). *The Problem* offers the critical thinking, *The Solution* offers the visionary thinking: between the two we get the best of all worlds.

Of course, implicit in *The Solution* sections is the *necessity* for solutions. This might need some spelling out. I believe that the Masculinity Conspiracy has been blinding us to the reality of what it is to be men and women. It's like being burdened by a cumbersome weight that prevents us from being as agile as we might otherwise be, but without even knowing the weight is present. When the Masculinity Conspiracy is exposed and inevitably cast aside, it leaves a gap, a lack of "something." If that gap is not filled, the conspiracy will come rushing back in as the only option on the table. That gap must be filled with solutions, as this is the only way we can reach our human potential that to date has been thwarted under the conspiratorial regime.

The thing about the proposed solutions is that you have to give them a fair go, even if they initially appear counter-intuitive. I'm a big fan of intuition: I employ it all the time. However, intuition has a near-fatal weakness, and that's when we are dealing with a subject in which we have little self-awareness. In our context of masculinity this means we have to be fully aware of how we are conditioned to think about masculinity. If we are not fully aware of that conditioning, our intuition tends not to draw on that elusive store of inner wisdom, rather upon the conditioning. So if I suggest a solution about masculinity that leaves you with a gut feeling of *nah, that's just not right...*, I want you to seriously consider the possibility that this is not actually a gut feeling, but a "conditioning feeling."

You might—after that serious consideration—feel the same, but it remains a useful exercise in maintaining an open mind. I'll keep on telling it the way I see it, responding to the demands of one charming woman who engaged me on an internet forum with the statement "give us access to the fucking information and do it for free." I can't, however, force you to believe it. Following conspiracy logic (again, in a somewhat tongue-in-cheek manner), the fact that you don't believe me is proof itself that the Masculinity Conspiracy has you successfully conditioned. Equally (and you won't get this admission in many books: the absence of which is also part of the conspiracy), I might just be wrong. I *have* thought through these issues for a number of years, including in a well-received Ph.D. dissertation, but nevertheless continually entertain the possibility I might be barking up the wrong tree. But, you know, I have a gut feeling that says I'm right... :)

The other thing to remember about the solutions is that sometimes they can appear almost boringly obvious. However, while something may appear obvious, it does not mean anything is actually being done about it. Indeed, it is almost as if the more obvious the truth, the more it is ignored (we'll get into exactly why this is the case later). I woke up rather late in the game to this fact. You see, I used to believe that if *everyone* knew something was obviously nonsense, then clearly it wouldn't be allowed to eventuate. Anything else would be an incredulous manifestation of collective stupidity. Then we witnessed the second invasion of Iraq. I used to shy away from making obvious statements because they appeared to me rather vulgar. Not any more. The obvious-but-ignored is the point of greatest importance.

There's something else to remember about obvious solutions. People often throw their hands up in defeat because while the solution is obvious, the process required for making it happen appears to be out of the control of the individual. A clear example of this is the eradication of world poverty. Most people can get their heads around the fact that there are enough resources on our planet to solve world poverty. However, it appears beyond the ability of the individual to do something about it, as it requires the international cooperation of governments, NGOs, corporations, and so on. The big difference about the Masculinity Conspiracy is that while its effects are of a similar magnitude to world poverty, it *is* possible to do something about it on an individual level. Indeed, in our context, the individual level is the main site of activity which, in turn, goes on to influence governments, NGOs, corporations, and so on. So by dealing with the Masculinity Conspiracy we kick off a chain of events that have genuinely world-changing results. I'm aware here of the danger of over-promising and under-delivering, but hey, the delivery is as much up to you as me.

So the solutions will be a mix of the predictable and the unexpected. Sometimes you will be able to accommodate them with ease; sometimes they will be hard to accept. This will depend on where you're at in life, the degree to which you've been conditioned into the conspiracy, and your ability to keep an open mind. For most of you, I'm going to completely subvert the way you think about masculinity, leaving it shattered on the ground in a thousand pieces. And what's more, I'm going to do it in such a way that you have no inclination whatsoever to put it back together again. Are you ready? Ok, let's begin at the beginning.

2: HISTORY

The Conspiracy

Remember, at the beginning of each chapter is the section called *The Conspiracy*, which uses one or two books as an example of how the conspiracy plays out in the chapter theme (in the present case, *history*). This section is about presenting the conspiracy on its own terms, rather than exposing the problematic nature of the conspiracy (this comes in the second section of each chapter, *The Problem*). The point of this section is to give a fair presentation of what the writers who exemplify the conspiracy intend to communicate.

You might think this was standard protocol when referring to other peoples' work, but unfortunately this is not the case. Writers who exemplify the conspiracy have a habit of offering a particular interpretation of the data to fit their own argument. So we need our bullshit detectors functioning at all times. When a prestigious writer communicates an historical "fact," or summarizes the arguments of another prestigious writer to bolster their own argument, it might be perfectly true; but it might equally be dishonest to varying degrees. I'll unpack an example of this later in the chapter. Of course, in all the books to which I refer there is a lot more going on than that which I discuss. I have, though, endeavored to be fair, but nevertheless focus only on the topics at hand, rather than summarizing the entire territory covered by the books. In this chapter I'm going to look at how the conspiracy appeals to history via two books: *Manliness* by Harvey Mansfield, and *Sex, Ecology, Spirituality: The Spirit of Evolution* by Ken Wilber.

Mansfield's *Manliness* was first published in 2006. Mansfield is a Professor of Government at Harvard University who, according to his faculty biographical note, "has hardly left Harvard since his first arrival in 1949" (you see, right from the start, it's tempting to put some spin on a statement like that, but if I did it would belong further down in *The Problem* section, for the sake of fairness).

The very first paragraph of Mansfield's book gives us a quick insight into his worldview about masculinity (or, as he prefers to call it, *manliness*). Initial exemplars for manliness offered by Mansfield include Harry S. Truman and Humphrey Bogart's characterization of Rick in the movie *Casablanca* (we may be getting to the point in time where such cultural references go way over the head of many readers). That first paragraph also claims that manliness "prefers times of war, conflict and risk." Mansfield believes we live in a "gender-neutral" society, which seeks to erase sexual differences, and in particular to deny manliness wherever it finds it. However, what Mansfield describes as "common sense" makes it clear that manliness is there whether we like it nor not.

Mansfield's manliness is about taking action and getting things done, often in a combative fashion. While those with a more evolutionary-biological worldview see manliness as simply being framed by aggression, Mansfield notes that this misses a crucial aspect: *thumos*, a term used by Plato and Aristotle to describe spiritedness which compels men to "risk their lives in order to save their lives." This more cerebral element to manliness feeds into two of its fundamental characteristics:

confidence and command. However, while *thumos* suggests something more complex and mindful than mere aggression, it is also a direct link between humanity and the other animals. Mansfield describes *thumos* both as "bestial courage" and "animal bristling," which offers an opportunity to risk and sacrifice oneself in order to transcend the self: a "faculty in common with barking dogs," as Mansfield put it. Humans may enact *thumos* with more sophistication than other animals, but we are common animals nonetheless.

This appeal to the animal kingdom and our biologically determined nature is crucial to Mansfield. He sees a host of "observable facts of plain biology" going back to the dawn of humanity which show that males are more aggressive than females: "men have more strength, size, and agility than females, who in turn have greater dexterity, delicacy, and endurance (they live longer)." For Mansfield this is all purely down to nature.

Also down to nature are certain facts about the way society has historically unfolded. For example, Mansfield claims that because men are naturally more aggressive and assertive "it is no surprise that men have ruled over all societies at almost all times." Further still, a less evolved aspect of this assertiveness—in the form of simply defending one's turf—can be found in various other animal species, which again Mansfield argues demonstrates its deeply ingrained nature.

The numerous references to nature require an investigation of the age-old nature versus nurture debate. Much of Mansfield's argument favors nature. However, Mansfield views this via the lens of human importance. In short, Mansfield argues that "human beings matter in the grand scheme of things." If manliness was down only to nature, then humans would not matter: their experiences would simply be part of the great unfolding of nature. For Mansfield, this denies human dignity and the spiritedness of manliness: "Hence nature must therefore be seen as a the guide for nurture." The fact that manliness cannot be reduced solely to nurture ultimately leaves the door open for humanity to define what constitutes the "human good."

Equally qualified is Mansfield's discussion of the public–private domain, which is often used to explain the differing roles of men and women in society. Men have historically been in the public domain (going to work and running society) and women in the private domain (having children and tending the home). Mansfield argues this distinction needs to function on two levels: it should hold true in the private domain, but not in the public. In other words, women should have free and equal access to the public domain, but in the private domain, we should all "admit" our natural sex roles, such as possessing manliness, with all its aggression and bestial courage. Mansfield speculates—following the precedent of history—that even with the freedom to choose, most women will opt for the private and most men for the public, which again asserts the "naturalness" of this formula.

So history works in a various ways for Mansfield. We have seen that he looks to our biological roots and commonality with other animals to understand the nature of manliness, which is largely characterized by aggression. While this is a comparison that could be undertaken today, it is essentially historical as it appeals to a timeless aspect of manliness that was present before the neutering affects of contemporary society, and which will inevitably outlive its contemporary denial.

But, of course, aside from animals Mansfield also offers plenty of examples of manliness performed by humans. However, this too is largely an historical exercise, given the neutering affects of contemporary society. As such, Mansfield makes frequent use of the classical Greeks who he sees as having a better grasp on the nature of manliness than contemporary society. For example, we read of the heroes of Homer who knew how to take a risk and do it with some honor. Indeed, the Greeks are presented as seeing manliness as "the main, or only, virtue." Or among many other classical examples, Mansfield refers to the Stoics as a foundation on which to build manliness, who offered a "philosophy of inner freedom, of manly confidence learned by living as if you were a prisoner."

Mansfield identifies more modern examples of manliness, but they are never truly in the here and now, or even real. Hemmingway's fictional characters and jungle-swinging Tarzan are offered; Nietzsche's superman makes numerous appearances. Mansfield's manliness therefore has a continually "not here" feel; it is, as he says, "unemployed," both defined by and relegated to history and fiction by the gender-neutral society, but waiting in the wings to return once more to its rightful place in the world.

To reiterate, Mansfield argues that manliness is:

- an aggressive, assertive and public way of being a man.

- based in biology and the animal kingdom.

- at its best in historical contexts.

- denied in the contemporary gender-neutral society.

The second book I'm going to look at that exemplifies the way the conspiracy mobilizes history is Ken Wilber's *Sex, Ecology, Spirituality: The Spirit of Evolution*, first published in 1995. Wilber is seen by some as a "new age" writer, although he doesn't employ the rainbows and crystals brought to mind by this orientation. He is seen by others as "the most widely translated academic writer in America," although he doesn't tick the boxes one might expect of an academic, such as having a PhD or routinely publishing with academic journals and presses. Whichever way, he is widely known as the preeminent advocate of "integral theory," which is a synthesis of Eastern and Western thought combined with the evolution of consciousness.

The subtitle of Wilber's book "the spirit of evolution" offers an immediate insight into the historical framework of Wilber's thought. Wilber adopts a developmental model where humanity (either collectively or individually) progresses through various stages, spanning history and each person's lifetime. As we develop, we "transcend and include" the previous level of development, so those historical levels remain of crucial—albeit transcended—importance. It is Wilber's presentation of the distinct evolution and character of men and women that is pertinent to the chapter at hand.

Wilber argues that men and women are generally defined by certain characteristics, and that these are shaped and confirmed by the roles men and women have taken on throughout history. In many ways, this is similar to the argument presented by Mansfield, but it speaks more directly to the notion of development and consciousness and, as we shall see, not only history, but also the unfolding of future time.

Wilber sees people as having either a masculine or feminine "type." These types are largely based on Wilber's reading of Carol Gilligan's book *In a Different Voice*, which was influential in the development of women and gender studies back in the 1980s. In short, the masculine type results in men focusing on agency and ranking; the feminine type results in women focusing on communion and linking. Mansfield also happens to make similar use of Gilligan.

Wilber views the differences between the masculine and feminine type as being based on age-old historical precedents that reflect the practical realities of being a man or a woman. He identifies a divergence of roles for men and women way back at the beginning of the agricultural period. Specifically, the introduction of the animal-drawn plow (over the hand-held hoe) meant that men's strength advantage made them the natural choice for taking on the role of "productive work" in the public domain. Women, on the other hand, retreated into the domestic labor of the private domain. While productive work (and consequently men) was assigned greater significance, Wilber argues this arrangement was reached by both men *and* women, "in the face of a set of natural givens."

This historical fact has significant ramifications for contemporary gender politics. Wilber argues that the whole notion of patriarchy—the oppression of women by men—makes no sense in this understanding of history. Instead, we should see society as *patrifocal*, with men's allegedly "privileged" position in the public domain not being the result of men oppressing women into the private domain, rather a *joint* decision by both men and women. For Wilber, any other understanding of power or focus in society would result in "the sheepification of women and the pigification of men," which he simply does not find representative of the truth.

So the roles of men and women—including the extra value assigned to men's productive work relative to women's domestic work—are biological necessities. The biological realities of men and women also have consequences for Wilber beyond the nature and division of labor: they carry on through to the evolution and nature of consciousness. For example, because men are more focused on agency and less attached to social relationships than women, they have a greater ability to see the "bigger view" and reach more developed levels of consciousness. (Mansfield makes a similar point here claiming more men than women would choose the public domain—with its "bigger view"—even when it is available to both men and women.)

Furthermore, the disparity seen in the historical split between the public and private domain (and the roles assigned to both men and women) cannot be fully undone. Wilber argues that even when we transcend the more worldly limitations of the agricultural era and enter higher stages of consciousness, "given the unavoidable aspects of childbearing, a 'parity' in the public/private domain would be around 60–40 male/female." We return again to the fact that it is biology that makes men and women what they are, and not only has this being going on throughout history, it will also continue in the future.

In sum, there are various things going on here about masculinity that are loosely shared by Mansfield and Wilber:

- Masculinity (or manliness) is a particular thing that has been in place throughout most of human history.

- Masculinity is defined by certain characteristics, whether aggression, confidence and command, or agency and ranking.

- The characteristics that define masculinity have a biological basis.

- The patrifocal nature of society (as demonstrated by the public–private domain) is derived from the natural characteristics and strengths of men, not men actively dominating society.

The Problem

My goodness, where to begin? One thing that both Mansfield and Wilber have in their favor is that their arguments sound perfectly plausible. After all, these are sensible-looking men citing equally sensible-sounding authors, right? Unfortunately, plausibility has to be one of the most dangerous things around. Not only does plausibility have only the thinnest connection with the truth, it is likely to be lazily accepted as true by those who are either too busy or too disinterested to know any better.

The most basic of assumptions on which these initially plausible-sounding arguments are based can be brought into question. Right at the start, Mansfield claims that manliness is denied by a "gender-neutral" society which seeks to erase sexual difference. "Gender-neutral" is more a term formulated by Mansfield than some commonly-held position of gender politics. What he is suggesting is that there is a large group of people (presumably feminists and those men who are too uptight to adequately express their manliness) who seek to deny that men and women are different.

There are a couple of things going on here. First, there is no single feminist position that can really be identified to which Mansfield can honestly make such a singular response. To fairly represent feminism we must acknowledge that we are talking about feminism*s,* in the plural: there are forms which celebrate sexual difference, and those which do not; there are forms which speak to all women, and those confined to a particular group of women, such as blacks, lesbians, working-class, and so on. To which form of feminism does Mansfield speak? By homogenizing them into one lump he speaks to nothing in particular. Of course, as a clever Harvard type (indeed, someone who "has hardly left Harvard since his first arrival in 1949"), Mansfield knows there are different feminist positions, it's just that fully accommodating them is not convenient to his argument.

But let's give Mansfield the benefit of the doubt on this matter. The second problem is that even if a "gender-neutral" society does exist it is not about neutralizing gender, rather neutralizing gender inequities. In other words, the gender-neutral society does not seek to deny differences between men and women, it seeks to deny people being treated *unfairly* because they are men or women. In this way, the "gender-neutral" society does not deny manliness in itself, it simply denies manliness being given some special position because it is enacted by men.

But here's another thing (which will be unpacked further in the *Sexuality* chapter): when we understand that the "gender-neutral" society bemoaned by Mansfield is actually about gender inequity, we see that far from neutralizing gender, the groups he rails against (feminists and flaccid men lacking in manliness) are actually about *diversifying* gender into many different forms. These groups would argue that given the patriarchal (or, for Wilber, patrifocal) nature of society, gender *has always been* neutralized, inasmuch as the masculine has been considered the default.

In short, Mansfield could not be further from the truth: it is *his* position which neutralizes gender by prioritizing manliness, and the *feminist* position that seeks to permit a genuinely "gender-diverse" society for the first time. Given, then, that nobody is really attempting to deny manliness, it makes the rest of his argument rather redundant. All that is honestly left for Mansfield to investigate is that the type of manliness to which he aspires *is on the decline*, but that's a different argument altogether (nor is it one that I can imagine being particularly successful).

For both Mansfield and Wilber the "plausibility" factor employs history as a legitimizing tool. The argument goes like this: "look, here's something I've identified that has been going on for a very long time, therefore it is true." Let's assume for a moment that the thing at hand *has* been going on for a long time (which is *very* generous of me). The thing to remember here is that just because something has been identified as a common pattern for seemingly time immemorial, it dos not mean it is "true."

There are two fundamental reasons why these patterns may not be inevitable, natural or true. The first reason is that there is a good chance we are simply witnessing the conspiracy at work (for seemingly time immemorial). It's a nice idea that somehow we had a period in history where things worked "naturally" and which explain the way things should be today and, indeed, should continue to be in the future. But there is no evidence to suggest this is the case. All we have is the assumption that because something has been around for a long time, it must therefore be true. Honestly, have a good think about this, because it makes no logical sense whatsoever: For a very long time people thought the earth was flat, but we finally wised up to the fact that this is not the case.

One particular spin on the "it's been happening a long time, therefore it is true" argument is the appeal to the animal kingdom. In this argument, certain behaviors are identified in the animal kingdom to demonstrate something about the "nature" of the human male. This is a common tactic in many books about men, and one employed by Mansfield. It usually refers to some member of the great ape species which is inherently violent, and uses this as an argument that violence is ingrained in human males.

Once in a while this animal kingdom argument is used to demonstrate other forms of behavior. For example, in some hipster circles in recent years the example of bonobos and their "casual" sexual practices have been wheeled out to demonstrate our "natural" inclination towards multiple and simultaneous sexual partners. The commonality, of course, between these appeals to allegedly natural types of sex and violence is that they explain (read *excuse*) largely male behaviors generally considered to be socially irresponsible. (However, there may be nothing inherently wrong with multiple and simultaneous sexual partners, but justifying this by appealing to bonobos is lazy.)

But it is a vast leap of logic to suggest that because a certain behavior is present in the animal kingdom it should therefore be found in humanity. Certainly, humans are animals who share a good deal in common with other animals (particularly other mammals). But we are so much more than that. Humans have a level of self-awareness that is (probably) not shared by other animals. Humans can strive for a greater good that transcends such primal behaviors. This is really what Mansfield is hinting at when he refers to *thumos*, but he is too wedded to biological determinism to fully engage with the implications of self-transcendence.

Further still, what of all those other behaviors in the animal kingdom that humans do not tolerate? For example, the eating of infants or one's mate after sex, which happens among some species? Clearly there are some "natural" things that even ape-like humans choose not to follow, which suggests the "human code" is at the very least partially constructed by humans, rather than being solely determined by biology. If this is the case then "masculinity" (which, as we shall see, is very hard to define) is equally constructed by humans or, as gender theorists describe it, "socially constructed." Which, of course, means we don't have to do it the way it has historically been done. It means, picking up Mansfield's point (again undeveloped because of his being too wedded to biology), that masculinity can be weighted towards *nurture* rather than *nature*. These initial points alone make appealing to history as our guide for masculinity problematic, to say the least.

In the previous paragraphs I've been working on the assumption that those (perhaps unwitting) advocates of the conspiracy have been identifying something that has indeed been going on for time immemorial; I've then shown that this is not necessarily a good model on which to base masculinity. However, it gets worse. Not only are those time-immemorial patterns an unsatisfactory model, sometimes they might not even be there in the first place.

For example, both Mansfield and Wilber discuss the issue of the public–private domain. Here it is suggested that men are better suited to the public domain than women: they go out into the world and do things like hold down jobs and govern society. Given that the public domain is more highly rewarded by society than the private domain, it is not surprising that men are more highly rewarded than women. That has a neat logic about it, right? Wrong.

The thing is, the public–private split (and with it the allocation of men and women to their respective domains and roles—whether they like it or not—and the consequent inequities of their respective rewards) is not anywhere near as natural as it might seem. For example, as far back as 1974 one could read Michelle Rosaldo's *Woman, Culture, and Society: A Theoretical Overview* which argues *against* the naturalized allocation of women to the private and men to the public sphere as a result of "women's activities" such as childbirth. In 1988 Henrietta Moore made a similar argument in her book *Feminism and Anthropology*. Plenty of others have spoken to this issue since. And there is literally a whole generation (or two!) of writers who claim that patriarchy was *not* a joint decision by men and women but a power system constructed by men, and that women are rewarded less even when they venture into the public domain in the same paid jobs as men. Again, just because something sounds plausible, it doesn't mean that there are not equally plausible counter-arguments.

The above example of the private–public split of course relies on differing opinions about and interpretations of historical and cultural evidence. I'm not suggesting that when Plausible Position A is refuted by Plausible Position B, the former immediately becomes untenable. I'm simply suggesting plausible arguments 'aint always as they appear. However, sometimes it's not just about differing opinions and interpretations of evidence. Sometimes a particular spin is put on evidence which results in our sensible-looking and prestigious-sounding writers being somewhat flexible with the truth when using the arguments of others to support their own.

For example, Wilber uses Carol Gilligan's book *In a Different Voice* to support his presentation of masculine and feminine types throughout history, which results in men focusing on agency and ranking, and women focusing on communion and linking. However, in the introduction to her book (in other words, *one of the first things she says*), Gilligan specifically warns against using her work as evidence to suggest that men and women are essentially different. The "different voice" Gilligan refers to is ultimately that of women and girls, which is "lost" in a patriarchal world, not a feminine voice that is essentially "different" to the masculine. To clear this matter up, and to ensure I wasn't projecting my own agenda onto this issue (and being equally flexible with the truth) I sent Gilligan an email outlining Wilber's use of her work, to which she replied, "I would not label agency 'masculine' or communion 'feminine.'" So what's going on?

Given that Wilber bases most of his understanding of masculine and feminine types on Gilligan, and that he is not too accurate (read *truthful*) about what Gilligan actually says, you might want to adopt that "hermeneutic of suspicion" to everything Wilber says about men and women stretching back through history. You might want to give some serious consideration to the idea that Wilber is part of the conspiracy. Thinking back to the previous chapter and Barkun's three conspiracy principles, it appears *that nothing happens by accident* (how could such a clear misreading be anything other than deliberate?) and *that nothing is as it seems* (the reality of the masculine and feminine types). What's left of Barkun's conspiratorial triplet is *everything is connected*. Here we see that the conspiracy/Wilber's presentation of gender connects itself even to evidence that counters the conspiracy: hijacking, appropriating, making itself plausible. Wiber's position is also connected in a web of writers who mutually confirm each other's position. This again gives the impression of plausibility and "evidence," but is simply a closed ecology of ideas which exclude those which do not offer confirmation. Ironically, while I am suggesting that the masculinity presented here is *part of* the conspiracy, this kind of closed-ecology thinking is emblematic of what Barkun would identify as the paranoid thinking that *identifies* conspiracy in the first place.

So please, whenever you read someone citing a prominent expert's work to confirm their own argument, be mindful that not everything is always as it seems. Plenty of writers are careful to represent the truth in this regard, but others are not. When this happens it is probably down to one of two reasons. First, it might be a conscious act of manipulation on behalf of the author: this is deception. Second, it might be that the writer hasn't sufficiently engaged the work s/he is citing to accurately represent it: this is laziness (or incompetence). Sometimes there is a third explanation of genuinely differing interpretations of a text or data: this is valid enough, but complex to navigate.

Whichever way, there is no easy way to avoid being misled in situations like this. The only way to guarantee that such citations of prominent experts are indeed valid is to go and read them for yourself. This runs counter to the way information is packaged these days, with its emphasis on sound bites, summaries and bullet points. Not many people have the time or the inclination to consult the original text to see what is actually being said by the so-called "experts." Unfortunately, those responsible for the conspiracy rely on the fact that not many people have the time or the inclination to perpetuate their campaign of misinformation.

If you go down this finding-out-for-yourself road it might result in the curious situation where you have *fewer* certain opinions. Basically, the more you genuinely investigate stuff, the more you realize how little you know, and the less inclined you might be to make confident pronouncements on any- and everything. My awareness of how little I know expands with startling speed on a daily basis. I'm not proud to say that I managed to get to about 30 years of age before realizing I didn't have a clue what I was talking about half the time. Only then did I start to see the true magnitude of the misinformation being spun in all directions.

In the end, once this method of misinformation has been revealed, it is the choice of the individual whether or not to be misinformed. Either be spoon-fed the lies, or not. It has become a cliché of conspiracy culture, but the "red pill, blue pill" scenario of *The Matrix* movie holds true here: "You take the blue pill—the story ends, you wake up in your bed and believe whatever you want to believe. You take the red pill—you stay in Wonderland and I show you how deep the rabbit-hole goes."

In conspiracy, the blue pill results in masculinity being a fixed biologically-determined aggressive condition that has been acting out across history. Believe whatever you want to believe. The red pill results in masculinity being any number of different things, and requires our exploration of Wonderland.

The Solution

So, what do we do about it? For all my complaints about Wilber, there's a good deal in his framework that points to where the solutions lie. Wilber sees humanity as being plotted on an historical-evolutionary developmental trajectory. In other words, things can only get better (or, more accurately, things *should* only get better: unfortunately, it seems there's no accounting for stupidity). Remember also I said that Mansfield cannot fully realize the implications of self-transcendence and nurture over nature implied in his own work because of his being too wedded to biology? This is a backwards-looking orientation, one weighted towards the past at the expense of the present and the future. Wilber does a similar thing: he aspires to the future (ever-higher levels of development, or what he describes as "altitudes"), but is strangely tethered to the past, anchoring his masculine and feminine types to the dawn of the agricultural era. This is not something specific to these two writers: it is common across the conspiracy and best typified by the constant desire to "reconnect" with more "authentic" and "archetypal" ways of understanding masculinity that is so prevalent in most types of men's movement.

Addressing this backwards-looking orientation is the first part of the solution. I strongly believe that masculinity has never functioned at its fullest potential. (For the sake of balance, femininity is also on shaky ground; but, as I've said, that's another book, which I urge someone to start work on right now.) Let's say it again for the sake of reinforcement:

- There are no halcyon days on which to look back.

- There is nothing to rediscover.

- There is no "authentic" masculinity with which to reconnect.

Does that sound a little bleak? It's actually quite the reverse. Earlier, to counter the argument that long-held assumptions must be "true," I offered the example of how we used to think the world was flat, but we finally wised up to the fact that this was not the case. Think about what that realization did to folks' perspective on the world: no longer would we drop off the edge of the ocean into some unidentified terror-void if we sailed too far beyond the horizon. Instead, we would go on to find new lands: scary—perhaps—but exciting, and full of the promise of new adventures.

It's exactly the same thing with masculinity. When we realize the limitations of our historical worldview we adopt a fundamentally different perspective on masculinity. We get to sail beyond the horizon and discover new lands—new ways of doing masculinity. Of course, just like the colonization of the "real" world, many of those lands are not new at all, simply new *to us*. These lands are often inhabited by people (the "natives") who are already living in different ways. As we extend this metaphor, let's not repeat the historical mistakes of colonization. When these "new" lands are "discovered" it is necessary to listen and learn, not to forcefully impose the rules from the Old World. As L. P. Hartley wrote: "The past is a foreign country: they do things differently there." Adopting this shift in perspective is largely an issue of managing fear: specifically, fear of the unknown. What we know is comfortable: that's why we stick with it, even if what we know has severe limitations. We have become comfortable with the way masculinity has manifest in history, which is why we stick with it.

But let's not throw the baby out with the bathwater. While appealing to history as our guide for masculinity is problematic, it nevertheless has great value as a guide for how *not* to go about the business of masculinity. In other words, we should look at the rather disappointing history of humanity, identify some of those behaviors which do not appear useful for the greater good, and simply state, "hey, let's not do that!" This is a genuinely good start. To figure out what's right, you have to identify what's wrong. This is not about "denying" history. It is about learning from the mistakes of history, rather than perpetuating the mistakes of history.

This principle also holds true with the issue of biological determinism. Rejecting the argument that we are bound by the same "natural" impulses as other animals is not about denying that we are animals. It is about denying that this animality is fixed and defines all that we can be. Sometimes we can even learn lessons of change from the animal kingdom, which is a nice counter-example to the kind of inevitably aggression-orientated stories peddled by Mansfield.

One interesting example of this comes from Stanford Neurologist Robert Sapolsky in his 2006 *Foreign Affairs* article, "A Natural History of Peace." Sapolsky was studying a troop of baboons in Kenya—subject to "typically" aggressive male behavior—who discovered a hotel garbage dump and began using it to source their food. Unfortunately, the food was contaminated with tuberculosis, which quickly decimated the troop. With the aggressive males—those who had most actively sought the diseased food—gone, the social mood of the troop became more peaceful, with only fewer and less aggressive males remaining. That's not the interesting bit though: I'm not suggesting we cull aggressive males! Once it had recovered, and new younger males began to enter the troop, *this more peaceful mood continued.* Sapolsky claims, "this troop's special culture is not passed on actively but simply emerges, facilitated by the actions of the resident members."

There are two things to be learned from this. First, in the case at hand, the "facilitated by the actions of the resident members" meant that with fewer aggressive males around, the females became more relaxed. They, in turn, treated new males to the troop more kindly who, in turn, felt less inclined to be aggressive (think of the implications of this for downtown on a Saturday night). There was a collective shift here—male and female alike—but the catalyst was a change in the male population.

Second, it makes it clear that new—learned—behaviors are possible, even within a context such as primates, often claimed as examples of how we are somehow fixed in our behavior and proof that a certain type of masculinity is not part of the conspiracy, rather a fact of biology. The solution, then, does not deny biology: it simply understands the limitations of a biological model incapable of change.

These lessons are implicit in the writings of both Mansfield and Wilber, but both are too backwards-looking for them to be realized. Mansfield believes in complementing nature with nurture (allowing room for human dignity), but is too caught up with biological determinism and historical models of manliness to follow the trajectory of his own thinking. Wilber is focused on exactly the type of development that I am suggesting is necessary, but remains bound by the historical masculinity his own model requires being transcended.

What both Mansfield and Wilber are missing is *room for change*. And here's the skinny: change is the key aspect of the solution when it comes to history and the conspiracy. We are not *defined by* history, *we define* history. Tomorrow, today will be yesterday. By changing today, we define tomorrow's history.

In other words, history is our framework. We dwell in the present, but are connected with the past in two fundamental ways. First, we look back on the past and can either perpetuate or correct its mistakes in the present (a no-brainer, surely?). Second, that perpetuation or correction in the present creates the past for the future. This is the real and proactive value of the hippy mantra "Be Here Now." Mindfulness of the present is nice; mindfulness combined with action is better.

History is the framework in which the conspiracy functions, and which it mobilizes to its advantage by presenting it as *defining* rather than *definable*. Within this framework there are individual sites of activity, which again are presented as defining but which are also definable. The first site of activity is sexuality, and that's what we'll get to next.

3: SEXUALITY

The Conspiracy

Out of all the elements of the conspiracy, sexuality is probably the most potent, the most regulated, and the most likely to challenge folks when revealed in its true Technicolor glory. Remember in Chapter 1, I wrote about how intuition has a near-fatal weakness, and that's when we are dealing with a subject in which we have little self-awareness? I said that intuition can easily be co-opted by our conditioning into the conspiracy. I asked that if, when reading this book, you're left with a gut feeling of *nah, that's just not right...*, to seriously consider the possibility that this is not actually a gut feeling, but a "conditioning feeling." I suspect that while the previous *History* chapter might have raised a few questions in your mind, my argument still sounded reasonable. I suspect you did not battle with a gut feeling when reading that chapter, but rather entered an intellectual duel with me: I made a point, you thought *ah, but what about* ... This chapter is more likely to get you in the gut, which is why I'm addressing it early in the game.

I anticipate two primary outcomes from this. First, you'll think what I'm saying is junk, and won't read any further, in which case I've saved you the bother of slogging through to the end of the book. No need to thank me, honestly: I value your time as much as you do ;) Second, if you stay onboard, you'll have a better position from which to read the subsequent chapters, which should enable us to genuinely break some new ground. This might not happen if I sat here anxiously wringing my hands, holding back all the juicy stuff until the end. Whichever way, in order not to shortchange yourself, you need to seriously consider the possibility that your response is not actually a gut feeling, but a "conditioning feeling." We're going to look at how conspiracy plays out in two books: *Earth Honoring: The New Male Sexuality* by Robert Lawlor and *The Way of the Superior Man: A Spiritual Guide to Mastering the Challenges of Women, Work and Sexual Desire* by David Deida. Remember, in the first section we'll look at the conspiracy on its own terms, leaving the analysis and solutions to later sections.

Robert Lawlor's *Earth Honoring: The New Male Sexuality* was first published in 1989. Lawlor shares some commonality with Ken Wilber—who we met in the previous chapter—inasmuch as he is looked upon as scholastic among new age circles, and new age among scholastic circles. I don't necessarily mean this in a derogatory way, as the intersection between these two domains is very valuable. Indeed, in some ways I inhabit this intersection myself: When I'm feeling particularly pompous I like to talk about, "bringing academic rigor to visionary thinking, and visionary thinking to academic rigor."

Right from the first page of Lawlor's book, we are connected with the historical framework outlined in the previous chapter, as he refers to how "ancient patterns of male/female interrelationships … can be enormously useful today." It is the use of "male/female" that is relevant here, as "polarity" is the one word that can be used to describe sexuality in Lawlor's book (and, as well shall see, also Deida's). For Lawlor, polarity is not simply a metaphor used to describe men and women, but the true nature of reality: he states, "we live in a universe that is completely dependent on polarity. The very energy that constitutes the universe is a high frequency vibration of pure polarization."

What this means is that the masculine is defined in certain ways, typically in binary opposition to the feminine, much like Wilber's masculine and feminine "types." Following the brain researcher Robert Ornstein, Lawlor offers the following chart to outline these polar characteristics, which start in the structure of the brain but which, he argues, also carry through into the body and sexuality.

Masculine	Feminine
Left Hemisphere	Right Hemisphere
Day	Night
Time/History	Eternity/Timelessness
Intellectual	Sensuous
Explicit	Tacit
Analytic	Gestalt
Linear	Nonlinear
Sequential	Simultaneous
Focal	Diffuse
Logical	Intuitive
Causal	Synchronicity
Argument	Experience
Perfection	Integration

Employing Jung's formula of *anima* and *animus*, Lawlor claims that all men and women have masculine and feminine elements, allowing for some slippage in these categories, but that generally men follow the archetypal masculine patterns, and women the feminine. However, due to distortion over time—most lately manifest in rampant consumerism—Lawlor claims our understanding of masculine sexuality has become skewed. For example, the type of masculine sexuality promoted through archetypes such as the Armored Knight (nobility and protecting) and the Divine King (expansive creativity and sacrifice) become "demented," and women become seen as object-like prizes.

In response to this masculine pathology, Lawlor calls for a balance, both between the ancient and more misguided contemporary visions of masculine sexuality, and also between the masculine and feminine. Indeed, Lawlor sees the balancing between the masculine and feminine as a cycle which defines history itself, inasmuch as in "pre-historical" times (or around 4-5000 years ago) feminine traits were more highly valued, whereas this became overtaken by the valuing of masculine traits: "This alternation between male/female dominance seems to be the dynamic that drives history, just as all progressive time alternates between day and night, warmer and colder seasons." Lawlor believes we are at the end of the current era focusing on masculine traits and are circling back towards the feminine, restoring balance—for a time, at least.

Through balance—achieved via an appropriate understanding of masculine and feminine polarity—Lawlor believes we find solutions to the sexual problems the world faces today. We hear from Lawlor that masculine sexuality is skewed to the point where it objectifies women, but this is only half the problem. For example, Lawlor claims that rape is partly the problem of masculine sexuality becoming too focused on aggression, but is also due to "the excessive sexual passivity of women" whose sexuality has been equally skewed through our patriarchal era, denying its adventurousness.

Lawlor offers the Australian Aborigines as an example of a tribal society that maintained the importance of the sexual assertiveness of women, resulting in a "deep understanding of the power and implications of sexual energy in the organization of all life." In the same way, while Lawlor does not see homosexuality as fundamentally wrong, he claims the "crisis in male/female sexuality" and its lack of balance means homosexuality has "grown to disproportionate levels in society and to pathological levels in the psychology of some individuals," presumably for those individuals who seek to impose balance via homosexual behavior "even though it is not a deep part of their basic nature."

The Way of the Superior Man: A Spiritual Guide to Mastering the Challenges of Women, Work and Sexual Desire by David Deida follows many of the basic tenets of Lawlor. Describing the "newly evolving man," Deida charts previous phases in masculinity, the first of which involved a stereotypical masculinity where relationships could be defined as "the macho jerk and the submissive housewife." Then came the stage that continues for most men today in which they seek to find some balance in their lives. Entering into Harvey Mansfield's territory, Deida claims this kind of balance-seeking has resulted in "sexual neutrality." Closely echoing Lawlor, Deida says balance is fine, but it must not gloss over the fact that "sexual attraction is based on polarity." Or, to give the formula a sufficiently Deida-esque spin, sexual relationships "need a ravisher and a ravishee; otherwise, you just have two buddies who decide to rub genitals in bed."

Deida notes that the masculine sexual energy of which he speaks can belong to either the man or the women in a relationship, but that one partner has to have it, and that is usually the man. In alignment with Mansfield's vision of manliness, Deida describes this masculine energy as being "mission, competition, and putting it all on the line (indeed, facing death)." Men with this type of energy, according to Deida, will always be turned on by feminine energy which is characterized by "radiant women, beer, music, [and] nature." The next stage for men that Deida proposes assumes "men and women to be social, economic, and political equals," but also celebrates "the sexual and spiritual passions inherent in the masculine/feminine polarity."

While Deida's point is that masculine and feminine sexual essences complement one another, this does not mean that this process is free from struggle. Indeed, the complementary process is largely one of negotiating power. When teasing out what men are actually after in their pursuit of women, he says to men, "You've had tit. You've had pussy ... And none of it lasted. It wasn't even that good as long as it did last. Your need is far deeper than any woman can provide. So what is it?" The answer, Deida suggests, is spiritual fulfillment. This fulfillment can be discovered via sexual relationships with women, but it is not the relationships themselves that provide the fulfillment, rather the spiritual gifts and awareness the relationships facilitate.

For Deida, achieving fulfillment and celebrating sexual polarity requires understanding and owning the natures of the two poles. In short, this involves understanding that women are chaotic (albeit lovely) creatures who will poke and test men to breaking point, searching out their weaknesses in the hope they will rise to the occasion (as it were), and prove their manliness. Deida suggests there are only two ways to deal with woman (and the worldliness they personify): renounce sexuality and "the seemingly constant demands of woman and world" or "'fuck' both to smithereens, to ravish them with your love unsheathed." Deida believes that not only does this bear witness to the true nature of masculine energy, but women also want it, as it allows them to be at their best: as Deida says, "If you want your woman to be able to relax ... you must relieve her of the necessity to be in charge."

But it's not all love and light with Deida: he also seeks to explain some of the more pathological aspects of masculinity and sexuality. Earlier, Lawlor suggested there are some problems in society that are caused by our crisis in sexuality, such as rape being caused by overly aggressive men and overly passive women. Deida also ventures into this territory, connecting not taking your woman "savagely, lovingly, and with no inhibition whatsoever" with a fascination with rape scenes on TV or at the movies. He suggests men need to own their "darkest desires," which may include forcing women to have sex against their will (a fantasy Deida claims is also often shared by women). Such desires should not be quashed, but appropriately contextualized: he writes, "the difference between rape and ravishment is love." Also part of this dark sexual territory is the "killer insider," whether it be unleashed upon a cockroach or home intruder, which women want to see in their man, and that men should fully own.

So, in sum, for both Lawlor and Deida masculine sexuality shares a certain commonality:

- The division of the masculine and feminine into polar opposites.

- The assigning of a particular set of characteristics to each pole (such as assertiveness to masculine sexuality and receptiveness to feminine sexuality).

- The need to fully own these two sets of characteristics, but to complement or balance them with those of the other pole.

- There are stages in history we move through in the unfolding of masculine sexuality, whether the cyclical nature of matriarchy and patriarchy (Lawlor), or a new level beyond the stereotypical macho jerk and sensitive new age guy (Deida).

The Problem

Lawlor's title *Earth Honoring: The New Male Sexuality* gives a clear impression we are entering "new" territory. Similarly, Deida suggests he is going beyond the older macho and newer sensitive male stereotypes to a further stage of masculinity. However, this is rather misleading. Indeed, every time I hear the word "new" in relation to men and masculinity, alarm bells ring for me, as it usually signals the exact opposite (the same applies when I hear words such as "evolve"). It's a bit like when you hear someone start a point with "I'm not a racist," you know they're likely to say something racist. Equally, I want to make it clear that I have no in-principle objection to the idea of "new" in relation to men and masculinity, as in many ways this is exactly what this book is about. The key lies in how we articulate that newness, and about being honest about what is new and what is simply a tired re-hash of the old.

In the previous chapter I had a moan about Wilber, but I don't want you to think I'm one of those types who sweeps away a person's entire corpus of work in one swoop, throwing the baby out with the bathwater. There are a number of points Wilber makes very well, and one that applies here is called the "pre-trans fallacy." In our context of masculinity, that old-school macho masculinity would be the "pre" of Wilber's formula (pre-feminist, for example). We are currently in the phase identified by both Lawlor and Deida as having rendered masculinity rather confused and limp, and both seek the "trans" part of Wilber's formula: in other words, learning from all our previous lessons, but progressing into new territory. However, in the pre-trans fallacy there is a danger that those who claim to be "trans" have *not* learned from previous lessons, and while they think they are in new territory, all they are doing is retreating into the old.

How we go about spotting that these allegedly new masculinities are really spruced-up old masculinities is not always easy. It depends largely on how much you know about those old masculinities, and whether you can recognize them in the first place. If you're an old-school feminist, it is blindingly obvious that when people start talking about what is "naturally" masculine and feminine, there is something fishy going on. However, for various reasons a lot of younger people do not have this awareness: either they have not been exposed to it, or they believe this type of critique to be old-hat (in some ways, it is, but it needs to be fully incorporated before you can move on), and listen in good faith when they hear about the "new" masculinity.

So, how do you spot this slippage between the new and the old? If you have the time and the energy, the first thing to do is to mobilize that "hermeneutic of suspicion" I wrote about in the *History* chapter: in other words, assume you are being bullshitted. Go and find some criticism of the people referring to the "new" masculinity, and see if this puts a different spin on things (and, for the sake of fairness, give the "old" critiques the same level of attention you would the "new" arguments): you can find a fair bit for free on the Internet. Of course, you'll find criticism about anyone who operates in the public domain (including me), but the point is not to leave people unchallenged. Does the criticism sound credible to you? If you don't really understand the criticism (which can often happen), how credible does the source of this criticism appear? Remember, when Plausible Position A is refuted by Plausible Position B, the former does not immediately become untenable: it simply means plausible arguments 'aint always as they appear.

For example, on a number of occasions throughout his book, Lawlor refers to Australian Aborigines as exemplars for certain sexual codes in society. However, Mitchell Rolls—co-director of the Centre for Aboriginal Studies at the University of Tasmania, Australia—sees Lawlor's presentation as an "Arcadian fantasy" and a "racist primitivism in which he seeks to permanently imprison Aborigines." Let's say you haven't the foggiest idea what Rolls is talking about. I'm not suggesting you should blindly accept it, but at the very least you might want to take seriously the fact that someone who undertakes scholarly research in this field finds Lawlor highly problematic, and also have a think about what else might be lurking behind his book. You might want to go and have a look at the types of texts Lawlor refers to, for example *The Songlines* by Bruce Chatwin, and see if that makes you feel confident about the foundations of his argument (Nicholas Shakespeare's biography of Chatwin does a good job of exposing him as a fantasist and charlatan, albeit one who wrote like an angel).

But of course it would be rather unreasonable of me to have *The Problem* section simply say, "go identify the problems for yourself," even if that is ultimately the best thing to do. I need to give you The-Problem-According-to-Gelfer, right? Well, here it is: the fundamental problem with both Lawlor and Deida is their insistence on reality being defined by polar opposites. This is another one of those arguments along the lines of "look, here's something I've identified that has been going on for a very long time, therefore it is true."

Polar thinking has been going on for so long that it has become highly naturalized and "intuitive": light/dark, positive/negative, up/down, man/woman. But because polarity is a "fact" of nature in *some* circumstances, it does not mean it is a fact of nature in *all* circumstances. Magnetism is a nice example of what's going on here. A magnet has a north and a south pole and, depending on circumstance, will either repel or attract. Magnetism as a *metaphor* has historically been applied to sexual attraction, but somewhere along the line its metaphorical truth has been confused with its literal truth (this is just one among countless types of polar thinking).

So, via this metaphorical–literal shift we then take it as fact that men (one pole) are attracted to women (another pole), or that a fiery person (one pole) is attracted to a cool person (another pole), and so on. But I would argue the anecdotal "evidence" for this simply speaks to our conditioning in the conspiracy, not any natural "truth." Once the conspiracy is exposed, *all people* are open to sexual relations with *all people* to varying degrees (men and women alike, of all characteristics): some of these sexual relations will be acted upon, others will only ever be contemplated, depending on the practical requirements of any given situation. I'll unpack this further in *The Solutions* section.

This polar thinking is not just about the types of people who are attracted to each other (via permutations of men/women, gay/straight, fiery/cool, or whatever), but the *values* and *characteristics* that are assigned to "masculine" and "feminine." Remember, Lawlor lists a whole bunch of these characteristics, following on from the left and right hemispheres of the brain. Deida does something similar with his construction of what defines masculine and feminine "energies." But again, there is no real evidence for any of this: it is largely down to an arbitrary allocation of values into polar camps. Honestly, tell me with a straight face: why are the values suggested by the words "time/history, intellectual, explicit, analytic, linear, sequential, focal, logical, causal, argument and perfection" masculine? Not only that, why are feminine values the polar opposite? Because polar opposites are natural? And the moon is eating the sun… There are two important things to keep in mind as we consider this issue: complementarity, and how we go about maintaining those values in an appropriate way.

In conversations about "new" masculinity there is a lot of lip service to balance: to complementing the masculine with the feminine, and *vice versa*. But balance is good, right? It prevents things becoming too extreme? Unfortunately, this is not the case. Based on the work of gender theorist Judith Butler, what I'm about to say might initially appear like an inconsequential philosophical/theoretical exercise, but it has significant ramifications. When we talk about complementing the masculine with the feminine with the intention of seeking balance and preventing gender extremism, we are actually doing the exact opposite: we are consolidating the masculine and feminine poles we are seeking to complement.

How? Because by complementing one pole with the other we confirm the perceived "reality" of those poles. As Butler puts it, "to be not quite masculine or not quite feminine is still to be understood exclusively in terms of one's relationship to the 'quite masculine' and the 'quite feminine.'" If you want to "complement" or "balance" those poles (in other words, abandon the extremes on which they are based), you need to proactively reject the concept of the pole in the first place. In short, forget *balancing* standard perceptions of masculine and feminine: instead, *change* the standard perception of masculine and feminine (indeed, understand that *there is no justifiable* standard perception of masculine and feminine).

Here's the second important point about maintaining those values in an appropriate way. When I unhook those words "time/history, intellectual, explicit, analytic, linear, sequential, focal, logical, causal, argument and perfection" from masculinity, it *does not* mean that I am dispensing with them; nor those words we also need to unhook from femininity. All those values and words remain on the table, it's simply that we no longer call them masculine and feminine; we no longer hold them in polar tension to one another. *All* those values remain available to *all* people at *all* times: men/women, gay/straight, fiery/cool, or whatever.

We do not need to think solely about *new* things in order to break through the conspiracy; rather, we have to think about *old* things in a *different* way. This is neither revolutionary nor traumatic, but a simple shift in perspective that can have massive implications for sexuality (and all things). Suddenly, we are not one of two likely ways of doing things sexually, but one of an almost infinite number of ways.

Before we get on to *The Solution* section where this sexual multiplicity will be further explored, I want to suggest one last easy exercise that can be used to challenge texts such as Lawlor and Deida's that I call the Mother Test. In order to undertake the Mother Test, you need to identify certain points in the text and read them out loud to your mother. If you don't have a mother, it could be any senior woman—either in age or achievement—in your life who you hope holds you in good stead. I'd like you to read out loud to this woman the passages where Deida writes things like, "for the feminine truth is a thin concept," and Lawlor that "ancient texts state that telling lies is an essential characteristic in female nature." You might also read out the passages above from Lawlor and Deida about rape.

How do you think that's going to work out? I'm not suggesting for a second that mothers are the bottom line for values in society: indeed, there *most certainly* will be things that need to be said that many mothers will not want to hear (like how they often perpetuate the conspiracy, for example). But the Mother Test is one of many tools that can be used in tandem with others to gauge whether what's on the table is genuinely a "new" (presumably positive) masculinity that you should throw your weight behind, and what is embarrassingly old.

The Solution

So, sexuality: what's it really all about? I don't know with any certainty *why* sexuality is the way it is. My aim here is to explain the net effects of sexuality and how we should deal with the hand we've got, rather than explaining how we got the hand. I know this runs counter to the message I've been sending about having to understand a problem before we can address it, but I think a bit of honesty is required here: the true reasoning for sexuality in all its complexity (in other words, beyond the base function of reproduction) is beyond us at the moment. However, and speculatively, I believe there are three main things going on behind sexuality, which I'll highlight in order to provide a bit of context for my thinking in this *Solutions* section (although certainly not meant as the last word on the matter).

First, while I have done a lot of moaning in the previous chapter about biological determinism, this does not mean I deny biology: it simply means I deny that biological determinism is *the* fundamental factor behind a lot of issues surrounding masculinity. For the sake of argument, let's say biology accounts for a third of sexuality. For example, in some sexually-charged moments I can literally feel parts of my brain start to operate differently from the chemicals that rain down upon it. It's a very odd experience, and to successfully navigate it requires quite a bit of self-awareness.

Second, I believe sexuality has a lot to do with seeking union (in a philosophical rather than physical sense). Spiritual people might understand this union as being part of a relationship with some kind of divine universe. Non-spiritual people might understand this union as being part of a relationship with some kind of entity greater than the individual, such as partnership or community.

Third is desire. If you don't rate desire as one of the most complex things on the planet, I suggest you haven't thought about it properly. Desire mobilizes both biology and the inclination towards union, but it is separate. In some psychoanalytic theories, desire is seen as the surplus to need. The object of desire is sometimes sexual in itself, but the desirous pursuit of the sexual can also be seen as a playing out of more general and unarticulated desire which generally cannot be satisfied.

With these three things in mind, how do we think more usefully about masculinity and sexuality? The most important part of the solution is to recognize that the idea of polarity is one of the biggest cons pulled in the history of humanity. We'll come back to this again in other chapters. But in our current context, this has a number of ramifications. In the above section, I outlined one of these as allocating specific values and words to the masculine and feminine, and how we needed to unhook these, opening up access for all people to all values.

The second fundamental ramification of polar thinking is the assumed gay/straight binary, which suggests that most people are either gay or straight (and that straight is the norm). Again, this appears to fit with all the anecdotal "evidence" on the table, but is it really true? One famous example that challenges this binary thinking is the Kinsey Scale. Alfred Kinsey was a sexologist who caused a lot of controversy in the 1940s and 50s with his work on human sexuality. Kinsey unearthed a surprising amount of what many at the time considered to be "unorthodox" sexual behavior in which people who were seen as either "gay" or "straight" often had a fair streak of the other. The Kinsey Scale put people into seven categories:

0   Exclusively heterosexual.

1   Predominantly heterosexual, only incidentally homosexual.

2   Predominantly heterosexual, but more than incidentally homosexual.

3   Equally heterosexual and homosexual; bisexual.

4   Predominantly homosexual, but more than incidentally heterosexual.

5   Predominantly homosexual, only incidentally heterosexual.

6   Exclusively homosexual.

While most people imagined the numbers would be heavily weighted towards 0 and 6, Kinsey discovered that at some point in their lives a surprising amount of people had sexual experiences (albeit often of a mild nature) that result in there being a broad spread across the seven categories. (There's also a eighth point, "X" for asexual or non-sexual). Certainly there are problems with the Kinsey Scale (it's considered quite simplistic by contemporary sexologists), but it still gives an indication that polar opposites—gay/straight, masculine/feminine—are not the obvious descriptors of realty that many claim.

This is not some "gay crusade" which suggests that lots of people are unconsciously living a lie about their sexual orientation. It simply means that things are more complicated than they initially appear, and that binary thinking does not do a very good job of representing the truth. For example, I'm happily settled in a heterosexual marriage; outside of this, like most men, it is women who generally catch my attention on the street. However, while I have never had sex with a man, I often find myself falling into flirtatious patterns with gay men, and now I'm a bit older, if I were single I wouldn't rule out some further experimentation on this front. I would hazard a guess that in the right circumstances most "straight" men would entertain the thought of sexually penetrating another man (albeit resisting being penetrated themselves, and there are complex reasons for this). I'm probably a 1 or a 2 on the Kinsey Scale, which I suspect is the case for most men if they had enough self-awareness and honesty to articulate it.

Owning such diverse sexual realities is not about sexual confusion: indeed, it is the complete opposite. While Kinsey suggested that a lot of this "experimentation" happened earlier in life, this may be due to our opportunities at this point, and that we are less conditioned and regulated by society's expectations (the conspiracy) than in later years. The more mature our sense of self, the more we are likely to realize our complex and diverse sexual nature.

If the dissolving of polar thinking in terms of the values assigned to the masculine and feminine and the gay/straight binary is taken seriously, what does masculine sexuality look like? In short, the answer is whatever you want it to look like: certainly not one of two choices, rather as the French philosopher Gilles Deleuze suggested, "a thousand tiny sexes." To suggest otherwise is to be subject to the conspiracy whose business it is to *define* and *regulate* masculinity, not to bear witness to the diversity of what it is to be human.

It might be that after exposing the conspiracy, the way masculine sexuality looks to you is a lot like that of Lawlor and Deida. This is an objection often raised to me: hey, Gelfer, if you're all about diversity, then the types of masculinity you critique are equally valid, surely? This is true, but the fundamental difference is that once the conspiracy is exposed, Lawlor and Deida's presentation of masculinity is simply one choice among many, *not a definition of what masculinity is supposed to be about*. That's a really important distinction, so if you didn't get it, read it again.

The real question then shifts from defining what masculine sexuality should be about to how to appropriately go about the business of masculine sexuality. We may end up with all sorts of interesting sexual inclinations after breaking through the conspiracy, but they may not all function well within the ethical and relational contexts in which we live. For example, I can imagine the appeal of polyamorous relationships, but the practical fallout in most stable relationships is destructive. Of course, there may be (probably rare) circumstances where everyone involved is on the same page and happy with the reality of polyamorous relationships, in which case I heartily wish you well on your journey.

We need, too, to be aware of the power dynamics that might arise in our newly-discovered sexual inclinations. One common outcome for men might be to opt for a "younger model" (whether male or female) as partner. The sexual attraction of younger people can be profound. Part of this is to do with the biological third of sexuality, referred to at the beginning of this section. Part of it is to do with death anxiety: of grabbing hold of youthful vitality which at once reminds us of our own youth, and provides a boost in the face of our own mortality. This is made all the more complex as we get older and achieve things in life, as younger people may be as attracted to our achievements as to our personalities (which can be very difficult to differentiate for everyone involved). However appealing such a scenario, if there is a power imbalance in a sexual relationship (whether through age difference or social position), it is likely to be inappropriate. On this subject I recommend reading *Sex in the Forbidden Zone: When Men in Power—Therapists, Doctors, Clergy, Teachers, and Others—Betray*

Women's Trust by Peter Rutter. Of course, there may be (probably rare) situations where a 20 year-old and 40 year-old are not subject to such power imbalances, in which case I heartily wish you well on your journey. These issues will be unpacked further in the following *Relationships* chapter.

A final point is the nature of "casualness" in sexual relations: a moral term if ever there was one. Historically, psychologists thought casual sex was emotionally damaging to those involved. More recently, studies have suggested this is not the case. However, it seems to me that if sexuality is indeed derived in part from biological determinism, the philosophical seeking of union, and desire, the idea of sexuality being "casual" is impossible. With these fundamental elements at work, sexuality can be nothing but "significant." If you disagree with this I suggest you examine more closely how these elements operate across all aspects of our lives.

One interesting alternative on this spectrum that does not get the attention it deserves is the choice of a period of celibacy. One reader of the previous chapters sent me an email stating that the greatest lesson of celibacy for him was "learning how to love a man and not have to possess a woman." I do not invoke celibacy in any way as a moral position, but a philosophical and practical one which is rarely mentioned but which offers a valuable space for thinking and growth.

Sexuality, then, is fundamental to the conspiracy. By giving disproportionate weight to biological determinism and setting up false binaries in terms of gender values and sexual orientation, sexuality offers a theme through which the conspiracy continually defines and regulates masculinity on its own terms. However, it is surprisingly easy to reject the assumptions behind the conspiracy's mobilization of sexuality and to open ourselves to multiple and fluid ways of being men and women, masculine and feminine. Once we have started to suitably manifest these diverse identities, we can put them to work in the relationships we have with those around us, the next contentious site of activity in the conspiracy.

4: RELATIONSHIPS

The Conspiracy

For many of us—either through a genuine desire to settle down, or the pressure of social norms—the sexual issues outlined in the previous chapter result in one place: relationships. Like all the chapter themes, relationships are another classic site of masculinity conspiracy activity.

Before we start, there are a couple of caveats for this chapter. First I'm talking here about the relationships that result from sexual attraction. In other words, I'm not talking about relationships with friends. That's not to say that friend relationships are free from the conspiracy (just check out the kind of quasi-autistic communication between some male friends, and the sometimes fraught friendships between men and women), simply that this is a topic for another time. Second, the two books examined in this chapter speak exclusively in terms of heterosexual relationships, which excludes about 10 percent of all men who aren't straight. Needless to say, the fact that this issue is not addressed in the books in question is a problem. However, the kind of themes I address in *The Solution* section can often be applied *regardless* of whether you're gay or straight.

There are two things you can deduce from that last statement. First, I don't think it's possible to imply much difference between men due to their sexual orientation, except that gay men have generally thought more about their masculinity than straight men due to the fact that they are under a lot more pressure to justify their existence and difference relative to the norm. Second, the fact that a "romantic" relationship between two men can possess similar issues as between a man and a woman suggests men and women are not essentially different. Of course, this does not mean that everyone is the same: there are differences *between* men—indeed, all people—but this is due to a variety of reasons: it is faulty to assume any kind of difference *because* someone happens to be a man or a person with a particular sexual orientation. In short, people are different, but not because they happen to be men or women, gay or straight. And when differences *do* appear along these lines, it is likely we are not seeing the result of *natural* differences between men and women or gay and straight people, rather we are seeing the conspiracy at work.

So, caveats tabled, this chapter looks at how the theme of relationships are presented in two texts. First is *Double Your Dating: What Every Man Should Know About How to Be Successful with Women* by David DeAngelo. This book offers a useful insight into the way the conspiracy frames the initial dynamics of finding a potential partner and establishing a relationship. Second is *Men Are From Mars, Women Are From Venus: A Practical Guide for Improving Communication and Getting What You Want in Relationships* by John Gray. A natural progression from the first, this book assumes you have a relationship in place and shows how the conspiracy frames communication when allegedly securing the longevity of a relationship. Let's first give both these books an opportunity to speak in their own voice before identifying any problems, which will take place in the proceeding section.

DeAngelo is an internet marketer whose dating products and particular philosophies about men and women have made him popular within the PUA (Pick-up-Artist) or "seduction" community (sometimes referred to as "The Game"). He writes on his website that, "I'm actually a pretty normal guy, who went through a point where I decided that I needed to get this part of my life called 'meeting women' handled." He writes that he spent a lot of time observing what men did who were naturally "successful" with women and that he finally began to understand the sometimes paradoxical secrets which attract women, and how this involves understanding what makes women different to men.

Do you remember how in the previous chapter both Robert Lawlor and David Deida suggested women had a natural tendency to tell lies? DeAngelo starts his book in similar territory with his first chapter entitled *Women Don't Make Sense*. He claims, "most women THINK differently than most men, and most women want different things than most men." This is demonstrated for DeAngelo by the likelihood that "women buy Cosmopolitan magazines, watch soap operas, and read romance novels. Men buy *Playboy*, watch sports, and read the paper."

The reason for this apparent distinction feeds back into the biological determinism discussed in previous chapters, as DeAngelo argues that "women's brains are wired differently from men's brains." Again, as discussed previously, he also feeds into the historic precedent to justify these differences stating that, "women are playing out a role that hasn't changed for thousands (or millions?) of years. These days the language and clothing are different. But it's the same that it's always been." Outlining the historical characteristics of masculinity, DeAngelo shares a commonality with Harvey Mansfield when he refers to "competition, adrenaline, power, domination... all the typical guy stuff. Incidentally, stuff that fulfills needs that most women just plain don't have."

DeAngelo also questions the value of monogamy as "men are hard-wired to look for sexual opportunities and seek out sexual variety." Again somewhat in line with Mansfield who claimed that the "gender-neutral" society seeks to deny manliness wherever it finds it, in his "it's OK to be a man" section, DeAngelo describes the assumption of monogamy as a "conspiracy against men being successful with women" which has been "formalized, passed down, and force-fed to us culturally by rulers, religions, and women for thousands of years."

The main drive of DeAngelo's argument is that men must seize the power and control in a relationship with women (somewhat like a mantra, a variant of "power" is used 43 times and "control" 31 times in *Double Your Dating*). Indeed, he must be in control of everything: "of the situation, himself, his emotions, other people, her... control of the entire reality that they share." In short, this means engaging a number of counter-intuitive strategies to attract women, such as avoiding being too nice to them (which is perceived as appearing needy) and rejecting any amorous advances which are not solely on the man's terms. This is encapsulated by DeAngelo's statement of "never give a woman a direct answer... unless it's NO... Never give a woman exactly what she wants." This is offered with the caveat from DeAngelo that, "I want to make sure you don't start acting like an 'asshole' to women. The masculine man says, 'No' to a woman calmly. The Asshole says, 'No' to a woman in an angry tone."

DeAngelo's claim that "men and women are different in many ways and that they usually respond differently to various types of communication" almost suggests that men and women are different species altogether. It is precisely this analogy that is extended and mobilized by our second perpetrator of the conspiracy in this chapter, John Gray, in his book *Men Are From Mars, Women Are From Venus*. As the title suggests, Gray's books is based on the metaphor that men are Martians and women Venusians: different species from different planets.

In Gray's story, Martian men spied Venusian women through their powerful telescopes from their home planet, quickly fell in love from a distance, invented space travel in order to reach the Venusians, and arrived among them where they were welcomed with open arms. At first, the Martians and

Venusians knew they were literally different species, and consequently spent a lot of time getting to know one another and learning one another's language and customs and, as a result, got on famously. Then the Martians and Venusians decided to travel together to Earth, where they soon forgot that they were from different planets and therefore profoundly different, and that's when Gray tells us all our problems started.

Gray suggests that life back on Mars was something of a paradise for men, as they only did things which came naturally to them, and which explain the natural tendencies of men on Earth today. On Mars, men had jobs where they could demonstrate their competence both through actions and the way they dressed, such as being "police officers, soldiers, businessmen, scientists, cab drivers, technicians and chefs." On Mars, men were concerned with "outdoor activities like hunting, fishing and racing cars." On Mars, "men fantasize about powerful cars, faster computers, gadgets, gizmos, and new more powerful technology."

However, over on Venus (populated by lovely women), Gray suggests, "everyone studies psychology and has a master's degree in counseling. They are very involved in personal growth, spirituality, and everything that can nurture life, healing, and growth." Such concerns are even reflected in the built environment, as Venus is "covered with parks, organic gardens, shopping centers, and restaurants." While Venusians and Martians were fundamentally different, Gray tells us that differences attract and that "in a magical and perfect way their differences seemed to complement one another." These, it seems, were halcyon days when Martians and Venusians knew who they were and each did things a certain way (halcyon days in which *men* and *women* know who they are and do things a certain way).

Back on Earth, this Martian heritage remains and means that men speak and behave in certain ways. For example, when a man gets stressed, Gray tells us he retreats into his "cave." So, when a man returns home from a hard day at work, rather than talking about his issues (which is perfectly natural for Venusians), men retreat into their metaphorical cave of silence and/or watching television. Gray says it is a fundamental error for women to follow men into the cave in the hope of trying to tease them out: men need to be allowed to emerge in their own time. Similarly, men must learn that women need to articulate their feelings in comparable moments of stress and to listen to these feelings without acting on the compulsive need to offer solutions (a distinctly Martian character trait, we are told).

In all the examples of language and behavior Gray investigates, men and women are at least different or sometimes even opposite to one another. Men, for example, are motivated and empowered when they feel needed. Women are motivated and empowered when they feel cherished. Men need to receive trust, acceptance, appreciation, admiration, approval and encouragement. Women, on the other hand, need to receive caring, understanding, respect, devotion, validation and reassurance.

Following DeAngelo's suggestion that women do not make sense, Gray suggests Venusians say one thing but mean something quite different, and he offers excerpts from what might be likened to the *Venusian/Martian Phrase Dictionary*. For example, when a man hears the words from a woman "we never go out," he should really hear, "I feel like going out and doing something together. We always have such a fun time, and I love being with you. What do you think? Would you take me out to dinner? It has been a few days since we went out." Without the *Venusian/Martian Phrase Dictionary*, Gray suggests men tend to instead hear, "You are not doing your job. What a disappointment you have turned out to be. We never do anything together anymore because you are lazy, unromantic and boring." By rediscovering that men and women are a different species, and taking the effort to discover each other's differences (and even languages), Gray argues that we can learn once more to get along and enjoy fruitful and long-lasting relationships.

In sum, there are very clear messages to be had about masculinity and relationships from DeAngelo and Gray:

- men like certain things, whether it be buying *Playboy*, watching sports or reading the paper (DeAngelo), or hunting, fishing and racing cars (Gray).

- men think and communicate differently to women.

- for men to be successful with women—either in terms of coaxing them into sex (DeAngelo) or maintaining a long-lasting relationship (Gray)—men must figure out what women "really" think and either counter or accommodate these uniquely womanly thoughts depending on circumstance.

The Problem

It's a cliché, but the old adage of "be careful what you wish for because it might happen" is pertinent when looking at these two books and what they say about relationships between men and women. Both DeAngelo and Gray have a particular vision of what men and women are like: they have certain expectations and those expectations are fulfilled. But the thing is, those expectations are fulfilled not because they are "real" or "correct": they are fulfilled firstly because of a confirmation bias, and secondly because we are again witnessing the socially-constructed conspiracy at work.

First, the confirmation bias. We don't need to unpack this too much, but if DeAngelo and Gray expect to see men and women in a particular type of way, the likelihood is that is exactly how they will see men and women, regardless of whether that is actually the way they are. It is absurd to claim that people are the caricatures presented in these books, and to suggest that these are "tendencies" which are *in general* correct is simply not good enough. Even if this *were* the case (which I do not believe), it erases all the personalities of those who do not follow such tendencies, which is a power strategy on behalf of the conspiracy to give the impression of its terms of reference being the only terms available (which is completely false), which brings us to the second point.

Even on those occasions where men and women *do* seem to demonstrate the characteristics outlined by DeAngelo and Gray it would be a mistake to say we are witnessing any inherent "truth." Again and again, we witness the conspiracy at work. The whole conspiracy—like gender—is socially constructed, which means we make it what it is: it is not "natural." *We* shape the masculine reality, the masculine reality does not shape us. It is crucially important to get this distinction in place in every instance the conspiracy operates.

In the case of DeAngelo, we witness the power aspect of the conspiracy operating with complete transparency. The conspiracy revolves around power, and one of the primary ways it does this is by co-opting men as agents of power, over both women and men who either actively resist being co-opted or whose social status make them less capable of asserting power due to issues of sexuality, class, physical ability and so forth (although power plays still happen among such marginalized groups of men).

Throughout DeAngelo's text we see examples of how men need to take power and control over women and relationships. This very proactive strategy on the part of the conspiracy is normalized by suggesting it has been going on for countless years and that it is biologically determined, when in reality it is determined by the conspiracy. More worryingly, DeAngelo's "seduction" agenda requires multiple sexual partners, which means he is casting his net of power as widely as possible, rather than within the confines of a monogamous relationship (which is bad enough). Note: I am not suggesting there is anything wrong with having multiple sexual partners, simply that there is something wrong with using those partners as a vehicle for exercising power, as demanded by the conspiracy.

It might be worth mentioning at this point that DeAngelo gives the impression that most women seem to appreciate his tactics, as demonstrated by his success as a seducer and the "honest" conversations he has with female friends with whom he shares his strategies. He's being completely open about his needs and desires and not lying to anybody, so what's the problem, right? The problem is that even if his partners give the impression they are ok with what he does, we must not forget that they too are under the influence of the conspiracy. Women are also conditioned in many instances to perpetuate the conspiracy, even if doing so seems a rather masochistic or counter-intuitive endeavor: it's a bit like how abductees can develop sympathy towards their abductors. Such is the sophistication and deeply ingrained nature of the conspiracy.

So, in short, DeAngelo expects to find relationships with women where he can assert power and take control and who desire a man who does these things, and that's exactly the type of women he finds. I would imagine the women who do not meet DeAngelo's expectations are either never approached in the first place, or simply tell him to fuck off (even if DeAngelo suggests this is a surprisingly rare occurrence). Consequently, the conspiracy's hunger for power is repeatedly sated and it simultaneously constructs the mythical image of sexually predatory men and sexually-cajoled women, rather than the more desirable situation of sexual relations that are equally filthy and fun but characterized by genuine mutuality.

Gray is far less concerned with power, however if you've been reading carefully so far, you should be able to anticipate my primary problems with Gray's presentation of masculinity. Sure, I understand that the whole "men are from Mars" thing is simply a little gimmick Gray has hit upon to describe men in relation to women, but let's not forget: it simply isn't true. Men *are not* a different species to women, men *do not* speak a different language to women. Relationships between men and women can certainly be complicated, but this is down to the complexity of communication between *all people*, not just men and women. In making it a Mars versus Venus issue, Gray constructs a convenient fiction around the complexity of interpersonal communication, not a compelling explanation. And in doing so he perpetuates the conspiracy.

For example, Gray states that on Mars it was natural for men to have jobs like "police officers, soldiers, businessmen, scientists, cab drivers, technicians and chefs" and for them to enjoy "outdoor activities like hunting, fishing and racing cars." But this does nothing more than demonstrate and consolidate that the conspiracy has allocated such jobs and activities to men. What of the men who want those things Gray allocates to Venus, such as "personal growth, spirituality, and everything that can nurture life, healing, and growth"? I guess those men are out of luck, because these things don't even exist on Mars; in other words, they don't exist *for men*.

So what does this mean for relationships? The sad irony is that while Gray believes he is shedding light on how men and women can communicate more clearly to one another and maintain better relationships, he is actually doing the exact opposite. By suggesting that men like certain things and communicate in a certain way, and that women like quite different things and communicate in a quite different way, Gray *does not* enable men and women with better relationships, rather he imprisons them to either Mars or Venus, both fictitious worlds constructed from his own limited imagination, which itself is saturated with binary conspiracy logic. Like so many others who speak to issues of masculinity, Gray responds to the intuitive feeling of dysfunction and wants to make things better, but unfortunately does little but makes things worse. If Gray didn't spend so much time trying to frame men's and women's experiences with his mythical Martian and Venusian complementarity, he might find that men and women are certainly different, but different *as people* more than sexes. If he saw and communicated with people as individuals rather than fictitious Martians or Venusians, he might not need a phrase book for translation purposes, but he might have to acknowledge that until that point his simplistic presentation of men and women has been shoring up the masculinity conspiracy.

Gray also highlights the issue of how expertise is constructed in the conspiracy, which we briefly touched upon in Chapter 2. The cover of Gray's book proudly carries the name "John Gray, PhD," which gives the impression that he must be coming from some position of research-based evidence, right? One would think (or hope) this to be the case. But if reports are to be believed such as Sarah Hampson's 2008 article in *The Globe and Mail*, Gray's doctoral qualification stems from a correspondence course from an unaccredited institution. Does that influence your perception of the position of expertise from which Gray is allegedly writing?

You may well be a sophisticate reader who wouldn't be taken in by such things, but plenty of people are not. I remember very clearly being in my early teens, when I lived in a simpler world. When I saw people in the media passing comment on something I would assume they were an expert, simply because they had been selected to comment in the media. If I saw someone was a "Dr," that person was not just an expert, but a "scientific" expert. Plenty of people think like this. It takes quite a bit of exposure to the world to realize that people get media coverage for all manner of reasons, most of which have nothing to do with their expertise.

It also takes some time to learn that unless they are referring to an area in which they have undertaken genuine—ideally peer-reviewed—research, most people who call themselves "Dr" are in no better position to comment than anyone else. You might even want to challenge *my* appeal to authority in this regard: I include the credential in the transparent hope of capturing a few unsuspecting readers and, to be honest, because I'm proud of my modest achievement. But I don't expect you to give me the benefit of the doubt simply because I have a PhD (even one from a "real" university!). Also, remember how in the introductory chapter I referred to the political scientist Michael

Barkun and his model of conspiracy thinking? One of the characteristics he identifies of conspiracy thinking is that it "enthusiastically mimics mainstream scholarship." Have a think about that the next time you see a book where the author is appended with a PhD or talks about their "research" (DeAngelo, for example, refers to his "research" six times in *Double Your Dating*, demonstrating a key issue of the conspiracy not only in terms of mimicking mainstream scholarship but also that repetition reinforces a guided perception of reality).

But consider too: assuming that, like me, you might once have assumed these people were "experts" but now know better, we see that there are always new horizons of awareness to reach. So if you think the argument of *The Masculinity Conspiracy* is questionable remember that, like me, you have been wrong before, but moved on. Whatever your opinion, if you think you have something completely understood, there is a high probability you are wrong. Consequently, in this book I am not suggesting that exposing the conspiracy is the end of the line, simply that it brings some critical focus to the issue of masculinity that is otherwise lacking: that focus can then be further tightened until it eventually approximates the truth, or acknowledges that there are multiple truths operating at any one time rather than the prescriptive mono-truth of the conspiracy.

The other tendency with a book like Gray's is to assume that because it has sold a gazillion copies there must be something of value to his argument. Otherwise, how could so many people be so wrong, or so gullible? Unfortunately, crap sells. Indeed, often the crapper something is, the easier it is to sell. I have a great example of this from my own chequered writing history. Back in 2001, I was sat at work reading a copy of *The Bookseller* and was shocked to discover that *The Little Book of Farting* had sold many thousands of copies in the three days before Christmas. With dollar signs in my eyes, I set about thinking up the most absurdly crap little book concept imaginable, and quickly settled on *The Little Book of Toilet Graffiti*. I went to a bookshop at lunchtime to see who published these kinds of things, returned to my desk, knocked out a quick proposal and emailed it to a few little book publishers. I sold the concept that same afternoon, which—as anyone who knows anything about publishing will tell you—is almost unheard of. Hot on the heels of this came *The Little Book of Office Bollocks* and *The Little Book of Student Bollocks*. Between these titles there have been translations into Spanish and Portuguese, and also an audio book.

What a success story. As the years have progressed, I feel confident that my writing has become better and better and the content increasingly important: however, it has also become increasingly difficult to sell to publishers. Now, with the writing at its most important, I find myself not even bothering with a publisher and giving it away for free. So, yes: when I see a book selling a gazillion copies it's certainly possible that it's very good, but it's just as likely that it's a pile of crap that plugs nicely into the oddities of the market with its strange desire for novelty books and, more importantly, a market which is under the spell of the conspiracy and requires books that validate and consolidate the conspiracy: neat, eh? While we're on this point, and because I am more interested in getting you to think critically than to blindly accept my argument, contemplate how *this* text itself echoes the same process, plugging nicely into the oddities of the market with its strange desire for conspiracy books: neat, eh? Are you wondering yet if you are being duped? By Gray, DeAngelo, me, or all three? I hope so, because whatever the answer, this it how we will begin to explore some new territory.

In sum, the conspiracy operates through relationships in DeAngelo and Gray's books in several ways:

- Both expect men and women to behave and communicate in certain ways, and these expectations are met, even it involves discarding those examples of behavior and communication which run counter to these expectations.

- DeAngelo's whole model is based upon asserting power over women, which is a key aspect of how the conspiracy functions (and by extension over other men who choose not to act in such a sexually predatory fashion).

- Both appeal to "research" or credentials to give the impression that their presentation of masculinity is of a credible nature.

The Solution

If indeed the cliché of "be careful what you wish for because it might happen" is pertinent to relationships, then the trick with the solution is to get the "wish" part right from the start. If the idea of women who speak in some kind of code is not appealing to you, then don't settle for being or partnering with women who speak in some kind of code. If the idea of the role of a man being characterized as uncommunicative does not appeal to you, then don't establish or allow that kind of dynamic in your relationship.

Assume things are not going to change for the better: generally, if things are not working out the way you want them at the start, then it is unlikely they will ever work out (indeed, it's probably going to get more difficult). This is less important if you are younger and floating around between partners, but there is some tough love necessary if you are serious about a long-term relationship: if these things aren't right from the start GET THE HELL OUT because you're going to waste a lot of your and your partner's time before baling out further down the line, or get stuck permanently in a relationship that is unsatisfactory.

Right from the start you've got to communicate effectively with your partner. Now you might argue that this is exactly what Gray is suggesting, but the thing is he is actually suggesting men play a cunning game: decode the Venusian language, pay lip service to its quirky requests, and everyone's happy (and similar tricks for women to pull on men). But in realty there is no such game: only honesty and transparency. Only with transparency can both parties communicate what they need and desire out of a relationship, and if you can't get it at least when you part company you know you have given it your best shot (it's very sad when people part company after many years of things not working out having never really communicated what they want: the other person may never have known and had a chance to meet those needs and desires). The paradox is that the type of man who communicates in this way is likely to be far more "successful" in relationships than with the kind of game-playing suggested by either DeAngelo or Gray. Because the conspiracy has dictated that men are not very communicative, those that run counter to this myth are highly valued.

Assuming effective communication, we then have to return to the issue of power. The previous chapter closed with the idea that if there is a power imbalance in a sexual relationship (whether through age difference or social position), it is likely to be inappropriate. As mentioned above, power is *the* key element of the conspiracy and it therefore actively seeks out such inappropriate relationships. However, I'm conscious of the highly prescriptive nature of such a statement which closes down relationships based on significant differences in age or social status. So while I think it generally holds true, I want to first open up a space for how such relationships might be able to work.

In short, if you're the significantly older or socially privileged person in a relationship, you have to find a way of giving your power away. You have to exercise what might be called a "radical vulnerability." If, for example, you have managed to partner with some young lovely who is in awe of your achievements, you will need to find a way to empower him/her. Maybe the stereotype is an older man who is successful but emotionally distant, and the younger partner is in a position to be the guide towards greater emotional involvement (assuming this position is vested with the same hierarchical status in the relationship as the achievements of the older partner).

Indeed, that radical vulnerability is probably the key to maintaining power balance in *all* relationships. It may not seem like it to most men, but they are largely in the position of power (even if they feel they are constantly being denied sex and nagged to do stuff they don't want to do). The power imbalance between men and women goes back thousands of years and even with the relatively equal opportunities of today this imbalance is still clear, most explicitly in the allocation of wealth and the split between the private and public domain (as discussed in Chapter 2).

Even progressive men have a weakness for glossing over this imbalance and repeating age-old patterns of power-grabbing behavior. Key ways power is wielded in relationships includes men assuming their work is more meaningful than their partner's (whether it be paid or parental/housekeeping), not consulting on decision-making, withholding resources, being emotionally distant, let alone more explicit examples such as physical and verbal abuse. Apart from physical abuse, I've done all these things myself (sorry about that), which just goes to show the insidious nature of the conspiracy, even if one is fully aware of the way it operates.

All of this requires making a stance which refuses to take on board these unfortunately too-common masculine traits. Back in the 1980s this idea was picked up by one of the few feminist male writers at the time, John Stoltenberg, in a book called *Refusing to Be a Man: Essays on Sex and Justice*. Stoltenberg's general idea was sound, but like various feminist positions of the time it needs more nuance: no male person should be expected to refuse to be a man (which is, after all, a natural biological reality): a better title would be *Refusing to Be Part of the Masculinity Conspiracy*.

With transparent lines of communication open and power in check, men should be free to then start being whoever they want to be in a relationship. Maybe men want to do traditionally manly stuff, maybe they don't. In our house, you will usually find me sat reading a book while my wife is up a ladder fixing something. At the same time we also fulfill some quite traditional gender roles inasmuch as my wife stays at home, keeps house and looks after the children while I "go to work" and "provide" in a financial sense. The point here is not that we have it "right" (we most certainly do not, for various systemic issues around the nature of paid work), but that men and women should be able to pick and choose between orthodox and unorthodox gender performances depending on how they want to live and how they feel inclined to manage the challenge of financially surviving in a world which has certain expectations about who does what in a relationship (especially when children are involved). It is important to note, also, that while something like staying at home to look after children may appear orthodox from the outside, the values within that situation may run counter to what many people perceive as orthodox (check out, for example, Shannon Hayes' book, *Radical Homemakers: Reclaiming Domesticity from a Consumer Culture*).

But there's a BUT coming up here. While the onus of responsibility is certainly on men to own their abuses of power, take the initiative exercising acts of radical vulnerability, and enact masculinity in any number of diverse ways, the success of such a strategy cannot be unilateral. Both partners in a relationship need to engage this process: in other words, women need to realize the role they often play in the conspiracy. As I mentioned earlier, women too are co-opted into the conspiracy which can result in them performing some unfortunately stereotypical ways of being a woman: indeed, the conspiracy *requires* women to behave in stereotypical ways in order to shape that "object" which is the "other" to men and over which they can assert their power. It may even be harder for women to resist the demands of the conspiracy as they are generally in a position of less power to begin with.

In short, any person with a male partner needs to let go of what they perceive to be the natural characteristics of their partner's gendered role. Sometimes this is going to be pretty trivial stuff, such as not assuming who is going to put out the trash. Other times this is going to be pretty fundamental stuff, such as not assuming who is going to "provide" and "protect" in a relationship. Maybe once this happens, such tasks remain with the same person, but if so it should be because they are genuinely appropriate to the situation, not because they are "men's tasks." This process is likely to be uncomfortable to navigate for both men and women: men have to resist manifesting the conspiracy, and women have to resist supporting men who manifest the conspiracy.

But once this sticky process has been completed, things begin to get interesting. Do you remember what it was like to be very young and contemplate what you were going to do with your life? A doctor, astronaut, or explorer? There was an extraordinary horizon of possibilities available to you back then. Much of the grief we feel as we become older is a direct result of those horizons becoming ever more distant, of becoming increasingly resigned to the inevitable "reality" of how things have turned out for us. But exposing the masculinity conspiracy puts us back in touch with that past potential. We may still be stuck shuffling bits of paper for a living, but we get to renegotiate who we are *as people*, and to be energized by the knowledge that the best is yet to come.

5: FATHERHOOD

The Conspiracy

Fatherhood is inescapable, whether or not you have any children. If you are not a father yourself, you have likely been fathered. And if you have not been fathered, it is likely that people close to you have been. For men with children, fatherhood is a potent site of masculinity conspiracy activity for two main reasons. First, it is a primary mode of transmission for the conspiracy: from father to son and daughter. Second, for many men, fatherhood closes down a number of freedoms that seem to funnel them towards ever-greater manifestations of the conspiracy. For example, perhaps they have to start providing beyond their individual needs, or find their values shifting with the new responsibilities of fatherhood (and the new pressures of the conspiracy). There is nothing about these examples that *necessitate* greater alignment with the conspiracy, but it tends to happen, as we'll explore in this chapter.

As with each chapter, I have chosen a particular focus or slant on the topic at hand that requires glossing over other aspects. In the following discussion of fatherhood I have focused largely on fathering boys, because I believe that the passing on of the masculinity conspiracy baton from father to son is most deserving of the time and space I have with you. That's not to say that fathering daughters isn't also a crucial part of the conspiracy. Just, as we shall see, conditioning boys perpetuates the conspiracy, so too with girls. As I've mentioned before, the conspiracy requires women to think and behave in certain ways towards men, and this conditioning starts EARLY (think about the myths to which you are alluding the next time you call your precious little daughter a "princess"). I don't refer to gay fatherhood, single dads, the way fatherhood shifts social dynamics with one's partner or other men, and a whole host of other important topics: but they're all there to be further explored. We'll see how fatherhood feeds into the conspiracy in two books. The first is *Wild Things: The Art of Nurturing Boys* by Stephen James and David Thomas. The second is *Better Dads, Stronger Sons: How Fathers Can Guide Boys to Become Men of Character* by Rick Johnson.

One more thing before we get going. Possibly more than any other chapter in this book, you may want to know about my "experience" with fatherhood. To be honest, I don't really think this is important in identifying the way the conspiracy works. However, I get this question A LOT, even when I'm just talking about masculinity in general: "have you got children?" It's as if I am not qualified to speak about masculinity unless I have children, as if that is a qualifier for "authentic masculinity." Of course, this is a shining example of how the conspiracy works and why fatherhood is one of its fundamental elements: if you have children, you "count" and get to hold the talking stick. As it happens, I have three children. If that means you give me the benefit of the doubt, great. But I'd much rather you questioned why that is an important thing for you to know. And now I am left with the uneasy tension of knowing that, like many times before, I have mobilized the conspiracy in my favor by telling you that I have children, and harnessing the small but noticeable amount of power this entails.

So let's see what these books say on their own terms, before some analysis in the following section, *The Problem*. Stephen James and David Thomas, the authors of *Wild Things: The Art of Nurturing Boys* are both counselors with an interest in boyhood. To demonstrate the above-mentioned significance that "being" a father has over "thinking" about fatherhood, after their counseling credentials James and Thomas state "more importantly, we both have skin in the game—with five sons among the seven children between our two families." It is clear before even reading their book that James and Thomas have a clear idea about what fatherhood is about: enabling the "wild" in boys and facilitating a noble warrior-like masculinity, as demonstrated by the two boys playing as knights with swords on the cover. Also of note, both James and Thomas and Johnson's books are written from a Christian perspective. I won't make too much of this, as most of each book speaks equally to non-Christians, but it's a point to consider as Christian writers tend to be more preoccupied than most about the nature of fatherhood, and there are still a surprising amount of people who are Christians and their values should be heard (and a tip of the hat to you if you're one of them).

James and Thomas take a clear developmental approach to boyhood, suggesting there are five stages through which every boy must be guided:

- The Explorer (ages 2-4). During which boys are active, aggressive, curious, and self-determined. They require boundaries, open space, consistency, and understanding.

- The Lover (ages 5-8). During which boys display tenderness, obedience, attachment to dad, and competitiveness. They require reprieve (not being forced into school too early), relationships, routine, and regulation.

- The Individual (ages 9-12). During which time boys are searching, evolving, experimenting, and criticizing. They require supervision, information, involvement, and outlets.

- The Wanderer (ages 13-17). During which time boys are characterized by physiological chaos, arrogance, individuation, and argumentativeness. They require other voices in their lives, understanding, and boundaries.

- The Warrior (ages 18-22). During which time boy issues are about finishing, being reflective, searching, being romantic, and ambivalent. They require a training ground, freedom, blessing, patience, and transitional parents (other mentors).

They state that these stages all have loose parameters and that boys will develop at different paces. Nevertheless, the message is this is what is "natural" for boys (and less so for girls), and that fathers should nurture these natural and particular characteristics. Specifically, James and Thomas routinely refer to biological differences between boys and girls and cite scientific studies that show boys' brains work in unique ways ("hardwiring") that fathers must address.

Each of these stages requires promoting certain types of values, points of inspiration or activities. During the Lover phase, for example, James and Thomas suggest watching films such as *The Adventures of Robin Hood* (1938), *Stagecoach* (1939), and *Old Yeller* (1957), which will presumably instill in boys the desire for adventure and the great outdoors. Also on the list are films such as *It's A Wonderful Life* (1946) and *The Princess Bride* (1987), which offer a message about appropriate family values and saving maidens. During the Individual phase, for example, James and Thomas suggest fathers should encourage activities including flashlight tag, paintball, flag football, night golf, ultimate Frisbee, wiffle ball, white-water rafting, high-ropes challenge courses, rappelling or rock climbing, and horseback riding.

All of these elements suggest that fathering boys is about raising a particular type of individual who thinks and speaks in a certain kind of way. Alluding to our exploration in the previous chapter, for example, James and Thomas mobilize John Gray's Mars and Venus metaphor to describe the "nature" of boys, which is distilled into three bullet points. "On the whole," write James and Thomas, "boys tend to be:

- spatial instead of relational (they understand the lay of the land instead of how things are interconnected)

- aware of objects instead of faces (they're more attracted to balls than they are to people)

- action oriented, as opposed to process oriented (they're oriented towards movement instead of toward emotions)."

Naturally enough, in order to nurture this essence of boyhood, James and Thomas articulate how men must be present as fathers, citing a number of statistics about how homes lacking fathers are more likely to: be thrust into poverty; diagnosed with asthma; suffer physical and emotional neglect; not excel at school; suffer suicide and behavioral disorders. Much like the mythopoetic men's movement championed by Robert Bly and his popular book *Iron John* (which I'll discuss in the Archetypes chapter), James and Thomas provide "a brief history of Daddydom" which shows how since the industrial revolution men have been progressively drawn away from their home and sons to ever more abstract forms of work, thus creating absent fathers even when families are ostensibly intact. This is what is known as the "father wound" that must be avoided, and recognized by fathers not just in respect to their sons, but also themselves, as identifying and reconciling with their own father wounds is an invaluable part of fathering.

Also akin to Bly's vision of the men's movement is James and Thomas' appeal to the initiation of boys as part of responsible fathering. They state that for initiation to be valuable, it must be costly: "think of a young man joining the Marine Corps. Once he makes it through boot camp, he will always be a Marine." They cite Richard Rohr's essay entitled "Boys to Men: Rediscovering Rites of Passage for Our Time," which claims that initiation must communicate to a young man that: life is hard; you are going to die; you are not that important; you are not in control; and your life is not about you. Such initiation, according to James and Thomas, "shows a boy what is wonderful and beautiful about life."

Rick Johnson, author of *Better Dads, Stronger Sons: How Fathers Can Guide Boys to Become Men of Character* treads similar ground to James and Thomas, but employs a slightly different language, the like of which is found in numerous conspiracy texts. For example, the first two chapters are called "Authentic Manhood" and "Authentic Fatherhood": the term "authentic" signposts a clear and definitive path for men to follow. While Johnson suggests that the primary point of (to him, divinely-ordained) authentic manhood and fatherhood is "living for a cause bigger than yourself," his more functional definition is one who leads, specifically via the term "servant leadership."

Servant leadership is a term popularized back in the early 1990s by Promise Keepers, a form of Christian men's movement. At the time it was felt that, for a variety of reasons, men had abandoned their role as leaders of their families. However, at the same time there was an awareness that leading families in a domineering fashion was ethically suspect. The term "servant leadership" is therefore supposed to be about leading with compassion. Servant leadership is about guiding the family through values, faith, discipline and finances. And while it is primarily a term used within Christian contexts, the general idea resonates throughout many conspiracy texts. For example, David Deida, who we read about in the earlier sexuality chapter (and who one might think is far removed from Promise Keepers) essentially calls for servant leadership when he make statements such as, "If you want your woman to be able to relax into her feminine and shine her natural radiance, then you must relieve her of the necessity to be in charge. This doesn't mean you need to boss her around. It means you need to know where you are heading and how you are going to get there, in every way, including financially and spiritually."

For Johnson, "fathering is at the heart of masculinity, of what it means to be a man." It is about protection: Johnson says that, "families are like flocks of sheep ... fathers are like sheepdogs, guarding the flock from marauding wolves." Indeed, the very presence of threats is often down to the absence of fathering on others: "young men, such as gang members, who are raised without the influence of older men often become marauding wolves themselves—predators preying on women and children for their own gratification." Effective fathering is described by Johnson as "father power" which, in a similar fashion to James and Thomas is capable of mitigating a whole range of issues that can descend upon a family, the like of which can have ramifications for generations to come. For Johnson, it is God who has given men this power. And only men are in the position to hand this power over to other men, or as he puts it, "masculinity bestows masculinity. Femininity can never bestow masculinity."

Johnson also reiterates the point about fathers being drawn away from their families by contemporary forms of work and living, and of the importance of fathers bonding with their sons, for which he recommends "camping, hunting, fishing, sports, scouting, rafting, hiking, biking, climbing, church camps, and other outdoor activities." Indoor types might like sharing hobbies such as "collecting (stamps, coins, baseball cards, etc.), working on cars or small engines, wood or metal shop, attending sporting events, household maintenance," and so on. Greatest detail about father–son bonding is left to a story about hunting deer, concluding with them gutting the animal: "blood up to our elbows, we basked in the glory." Keen also to encourage reading, Johnson recommends books about founding fathers, pioneers, frontiersmen, cowboys, soldiers, and athletes.

In sum, there are very clear messages to be had about masculinity and fatherhood from James, Thomas and Johnson:

- Fathers must nurture specific sets of behaviors at different times of a boy's life.

- Those behaviors are hardwired and are focused largely on outdoor activities and what might be described as stereotypical ways of doing masculinity.

- Fathers should bond with their boys over such activities, perhaps even via some form of difficult initiation in order to turn boys into men.

- Fathering is about leading and protecting the whole family, wives and children alike.

- Boys without fathers suffer a father wound and are more likely to perform poorly in society.

The Problem

The primary problem with these two books is the expectations they outline. For example, James and Thomas are developmentalists, which means they expect boys to develop through distinct phases on their journey to adulthood. Certainly, they at least pay lip service to the fact that not all boys will go through the same stages of development at the same time, and that the stages are fluid in nature. However, there remains a clear assumption that *in general* boys develop in certain ways. The problem here, of course, is that such assumptions establish a norm, and if boys do not adhere to it then they become, by default, *ab*normal.

The other thing to notice about these developmental stages is that they themselves are constructed via the lens of conspiracy assumptions about masculinity. We read of the Explorer, the Individual, the Wanderer and the Warrior. Note how all these are typical conspiracy-like signifiers for masculinity. Now, the logic of the conspiracy will tell us this is because *that's the way masculinity is*. But even if we acknowledge that there *are* distinct stages in boys' development, my feeling is that if you looked at the range of behaviors demonstrated in any one of those stages there would be other ways of describing them that did not employ such explicit "masculine" assumptions. For example, if instead of "Explorer," we had "discovering connections between things" we have something that works along similar lines, but with a less mono-gendered nature (connections typically being considered a "feminine" trait). In a similar way, the "Individual" could be "discovering self," the "Wanderer" and could be "developing intuition." I'm just thinking on the fly with these examples, but no doubt there are a variety of different ways such stages could be described if we think creatively, and many of them would not feed into those assumptions about masculinity.

And, of course, those stages may just not exist with the certainty these authors suggest. Just like the problem with Venus and Mars, when we come to expect a certain thing, we tend to start seeing it, whether or not it's really there. It is a useful exercise to consider this on a continual basis with all things: am I seeing things the way they really are, or am I seeing them the way I am being told to see them? Keep that in mind the next time you watch the news, have a meeting, go on a date or even shopping. You might be surprised how easy it is to scratch away the veneer of consensus reality and expose the "real" world beneath. This is where the great explorations of the 21st century will be: not in distant and extraordinary places, but in our immediate and everyday surrounds, but viewed minus the conspiratorial blinkers.

If these stages are problematic then so, of course, are the suggestions offered by these authors about how to best serve them. Certainly, if a stereotypically masculine stage is identified, then all those suggestions about outdoor activities and watching movies about cowboys and Indians seem appropriate. But if a stage is defined in altogether different ways, then equally different suggestions are required. You might need activities that engage emotional rather than spatial intelligence, and movies the feed aspirations to be a designer or priest rather than a forest ranger. Instead of following a prescriptive path about boyhood, it will be necessary to actually get to know the boy in question and respond to rather than shape his characteristics. The alternative, as suggested by the conspiracy, is a self-fulfilling prophecy: either typical masculine traits are mapped on to the boy to the point where he feels these are "natural" interests (thus perpetuating the conspiracy), or the boy is alienated by this process and becomes one of the less powerful men who are dominated in the conspiracy (and given the conspiracy requires such people over which to assert power, this also perpetuates the conspiracy).

The suggestions of what is appropriate fathering to boys also manifest in James and Thomson's call for initiation, which is generally assumed to be a difficult and painful ritual that bestows identify upon a boy and enables his passage into maturity. Many men's movement writers who appeal to initiation refer to traditional or tribal societies where such rituals exist to demonstrate how this is a natural process, the like of which averts the kinds of masculinity "crises" we experience today in the developed world.

There are three significant problems with such a call to initiation. First, it is absurd to say that because tribal societies do something a certain way that we should also do it: would the same people who claim this also suggest we revert to tribal forms of technology and medicine? I don't think so. Even if such rituals work great in tribal societies, it does not mean they will work great for western urban societies: for initiation to work we would need rituals that are context-specific. Second, why must initiation be a hazardous and painful ritual? If ritual must exist, then there is no reason why it should adhere to typically masculine traits such as hazard and pain. Initiation rituals should be *learning* rituals, and there aren't that many educationalists around these days who advocate learning through hazard and pain.

The third problem gets right to the heart of the conspiracy. We are told that the point of initiation is essentially about bestowing mature masculine identity on a boy, of securing his "self" and welcoming him into the society of authentic manhood. However, I would argue that paradoxically, initiation does *exactly the opposite*. Instead of bestowing some form of unique self upon a boy, initiation demands that a boy conform to the social codes of authentic manhood, abandoning the unique (and natural) self he already possesses as a boy. Initiation, then, is really a process in which a boy is co-opted into the values of the society in general and the conspiracy in particular. Initiation is nothing short of being sold into slavery, but it is done with such extraordinary finesse that those who have been enslaved believe they have been welcomed into some exclusive club. This sleight of hand is one of the key elements of the conspiracy and will be explored in greater depth in the concluding chapter.

Once a man has been co-opted into a peculiar set of values and made to feel as if he is very special as a result, it becomes easy to make all sorts of equally peculiar suggestions to him and for them to be accepted uncritically. One such example of this is the above-mentioned appeal to servant leadership, in which a man leads his family, but in a supposedly benign fashion. I find it a remarkable achievement on behalf of the conspiracy that in a society which has experienced a number of decades of women's empowerment, men can still get away with asking for (and receiving) the leadership of a family, as if his partner is less capable of such leadership.

In the context of Johnson's Christian worldview, this right to leadership is divinely-ordained, but of course it is far more likely that this "right" is simply a power play asserted by the conspiracy (I strongly believe this causality is easier to quantify than God's will, even though I have a spiritual worldview myself!). I mentioned earlier that Deida makes a similar call from a secular perspective, for men to "relieve her of the necessity to be in charge." For Deida, this is not divinely-ordained, rather the masculine "gift": again, it seems easier to simply identify this as

82

the conspiracy at work, rather than some mysterious "gift" that has been bestowed by nature upon men alone.

This line of thinking positions a specific form of masculinity in general, and fatherhood in particular, as being the most privileged form of agency in society. The authors referred to in this chapter continue this by outlining all the ills that descend upon children when fathers are absent, such as poorer health and education. However, with conspiracy claims it is always important to look beyond the supplied reasoning, For example, the claim about health and housing certainly sounds plausible, but is it down to the lack of a father in the home, or the lack of a father's income (which has a habit of exiting the family home along with the father). If health and education were less tied by society to financial stability (or if financial stability were less tied to men), then perhaps the "father factor" would be less significant here.

This is not to say that fathers are unimportant. Of course, fathers are crucial, but the issue here is one of the loving, support and resources provided within the home rather than a "man" performing "fatherhood." I would be willing to bet, for example, that the health and education of children brought up by loving and financially stable lesbian mothers is better than a loving single parent of either sex who is financially stretched and comparable to a loving family with both a mother and a father with equal access to resources. This is a classic example of the economic basis for the conspiracy, which we will get to later in the book. At the end of the day it is fully resourced *parenting* that is crucial (financially, emotionally, spiritually and culturally), not *fathering* (or for that matter, mothering). Again, do not hear me say here that fathers are not important. All fathers are important, but it is the parenting they provide that is important, not something specific to do with that parenting coming from a man (and again, this goes for mothering too: once childbirth and breastfeeding is over there is nothing uniquely "valuable" about mothering; the value is in the parenting).

So to recap, there are several initial problems with the way James, Thomas and Johnson present fatherhood:

- The assumption that boys develop through particular stages is prescriptive and focused around stereotypically masculine themes: this either conditions boys to perpetuate those themes or suggests they are in some way abnormal.

- Hazardous or painful initiation that is supposedly beneficial to boys has no real context in western society, and can be seen more as a way of making boys conform to social values than offering a mature masculine identity.

- Servant leadership is simply another site where the conspiracy asserts power rather than being something "natural" or "divinely ordained."

- Lack of fathering does not necessarily cause the problems that many fathering advocates suggest, rather lack of *parenting*.

The Solution

Clearly, the solutions to fathering in ways that counter the conspiracy are extraordinarily complex. The above sections barely expose the tip of the iceberg in terms of the issues involved. However, I want to identify two paths of exploration that I think are the most important, both within themselves, and also in an attempt to indicate the breadth of the solution. The first path frames fatherhood as being focused on the child and how we might resist conditioning the child into the conspiracy. The second path frames fatherhood as being focused on the father and how we might resist further conditioning the man into the conspiracy.

In his recent book *Ethics in Light of Childhood*, ethicist John Wall proposes the concept of "childism," which prioritizes the experiences of the child. In just the same way that other *isms* such as feminism acknowledge the unique ways in which women have power asserted over them, so too childism acknowledges that children form a distinct (although not homogenous) social group that is subject to certain power plays. Wall notes that, "Children are a third of all humanity. Yet all too often children are considered merely undeveloped adults, passive recipients of care, occupying a separate innocence, or, perhaps, in need of being civilized." I want to co-opt Wall's argument as the basis for a counter-conspiratorial strategy (although not necessarily one that his sophisticated ethical framework would want to accommodate!).

The conspiracy views children, as Wall suggests, as undeveloped adults in need of civilization. Specifically, via a particular form of fatherhood, the conspiracy mobilizes men to condition children into the values of the conspiracy. Conspiratorial fatherhood uses aspirations to initiation, or activities and movies "appropriate" to a boy's stage of development as a way of making children conform. Viewed via the lens of the conspiracy, a father *unwittingly* asks the question, "What do I need to do in order to serve the needs of the conspiracy?" Viewed via the lens of childism, a father *proactively* asks the question, "What do I need to do in order to serve the needs of the child?" The conspiracy would suggest these two questions are largely the same, but this is most certainly not the case; indeed, the two are largely at odds.

The real challenge of counter-conspiratorial fathering is that it cannot be successfully done without first owning how the conspiracy has already shaped fathers who seek to be counter-conspiratorial (through the kind of themes addressed in the History, Sexuality and Relationships chapters). This is a particularly daunting fact if you are only just waking up to your own conditioning by the conspiracy and also happen to be a father, as you are faced with the double challenge of unpicking both your own and your child's conditioning (for which, unfortunately, you are largely responsible). The good news is that there is a mutually beneficial process at work here: a father initially identifies that he has been duped by the conspiracy and that in turn he has passed the conspiracy on to his child; however, by actively undoing the child's conditioning, new layers of his own conditioning become apparent to him, which he can then reflect back to the child. Think of fatherhood as an accelerant: it speeds up and intensifies the potency of the conspiracy when it goes unchecked, but also has the potential to speed up and intensify its rejection.

As with other chapters, the solutions appear almost simplistic. There is nothing in the conspiracy or its rejection that is particularly complicated. The conspiracy is a power system that employs various themes to leverage that power: each chapter you are reading is looking at this exact same thing from a different angle (you have probably already noticed a certain predictable repetition in this text as a result). The solution is about waking up to the fact that the conspiracy has being going on for so long that it has become highly naturalized, and simply choosing not to be part of it. It's not the first time that I've evoked the image of slavery in this chapter, but it continues to be apt. For a long time people thought it was natural to enslave people, but once the (really rather simple) ethical implications of this had been fully outlined and politicized, it became a difficult position to justify.

Counter-conspiratorial fathering is simply about choosing not to put the perpetuation of conspiratorial values first, and instead promoting the values of the child. And here's the key point, in just the same way as the conspiracy tells us the supposed nature of the values that define masculinity, so too childhood. And just as countering the conspiracy is about realizing that there *are no certain values* that define masculinity, so too childhood. There are *very few* values that are "appropriate" to childhood, and those (such as love and support) work equally well for boys and girls.

There is no "way" to bring up "boys," as if they are a single type of thing with a single set of needs. I always find the idea of "special needs" (usually applied to physical and mental "disabilities") in respect to children truly bizarre, as if there was a child that *did not* have special needs. *All children are "special needs" children.* Further still, after that realization I would then reject the term "special needs" (including for those perceived to be disabled), and say all children have *different needs*, period. That is the key to counter-conspiratorial fathering: difference; that is the key to counter-conspiratorial masculinity. I am not talking about treating all children the same (the kind of "gender-neutral society" bemoaned by Harvey Mansfield in the History chapter), rather treating all children in a way that meets their different needs. There is nothing neutralizing about this: we return to the value of multiplicity, rather than the prescriptive nature of thinking about boys' and girls' needs in terms of binary gendered characteristics.

Focusing on the genuine needs of the child rather than projecting conspiratorial values onto them is one crucial part of the equation, but I want to conclude with a focus on fathers and their sense of self. Now there will no doubt be a lot of people out there (particularly women) who think that given the prevalence of absent fathers—both literally so, and those emotionally withdrawn within the home—that their sense of self is already well established and prioritized over all things. But hear me out.

I suspect that in the conspiracy fatherhood has the potential to function in a dissociative manner. In much the same way that initiation does not, as it is claimed, bestow a sense of identify upon a boy but instead erases it through conformity, so too fatherhood (at least a particular form of fatherhood as advocated by the conspiracy). It is a pattern I have identified amongst both those around me and myself: that the "responsibilities of fatherhood" (providing, and so forth) have an unnerving habit of not, as one would hope, developing the sense of self, rather eroding it. This process is identifiable in the conservative drift that appears to take place upon the values of many men as they spend more time as fathers, a drift in values that more often than not serves the conspiracy.

The clichéd example of this would be a young, relatively free-thinking man who settles down and has a family. Let's call him, I dunno, Joseph Helfer. Now Joseph starts out with good intentions about resisting the conservative drift that seems to take place in the fathers he sees around him, however his resolve is soon tested. In order to pay the mortgage and support a wife and three children he has to ensure financial stability, and the only apparent way of achieving this is by doing what is expected of him and staying put in a sensible job (and behaving in it like a sensible man).

Now the sensible job is a challenge for Joseph in two ways. First, maintaining it requires perpetuating what he perceives to be unsavory values to such a degree that he no longer knows if he is secretly resisting or perpetuating them. Second, maintaining it requires abandoning certain dreams, the pursuit of which is deemed too risky. The net result is resentment, both of the system that is co-opting him, and the family that—through its need for financial support—requires him to be in the system in the first place. Both these challenges have a dissociative effect on Joseph, removing him from his original sense of self, from his ability to sufficiently critique the conspiracy, and thus his ability to see how the conspiracy is slowly claiming him for its own and perpetuating its values in any number of ways. Conspiracy by a thousand cuts.

I would argue that the absence of fathers—both literally so, and those emotionally withdrawn within the home—can be understood *in some circumstances* not as the result of selfishness on behalf of those men, rather their *lack* of self. It is the conspiracy that demands that fatherhood functions in a particular kind of way and which divorces men from themselves *before* their wives. It is the trauma of a man either consciously realizing (or, just as potently, unconsciously feeling) that he is not the person he used to be that puts him into self-imposed exile, or to act out in the kind of destructive ways that result in him being exiled by his partner. These are the hidden casualties of the conspiracy: not capable of being winners on the conspiracy's terms, yet not capable of proactively resisting the conspiracy.

Do not hear me say this is a problem due to wives or families: it is a problem with the way the conspiracy demands men to function in society. It is crucial that the "blame" be correctly located, which is where a lot of men's rights advocates go wrong: the problems men face have little to do with women, their advancements and characteristics; it has a lot to do with the conspiracy which traps men and women in different ways.

The solution, then, relies not just on focusing on the genuine needs of the child, but also the genuine needs of the father. Fathers must be true to who they are (mothers too, of course). If, as a result of fatherhood, men enter a new sense of self that is both more elevated and satisfying than their previous experience, everyone's a winner: I know this happens a lot, and it's great to see. If, on the other hand, fatherhood (or at least those expectations imposed by the conspiracy) proves a fatal blow to one's sense of self, changes are necessary. Given there are only two likely outcomes from this (men are either fully engulfed or mercilessly rejected by the conspiracy), it is in everyone's interest to ensure these men remain connected with what they perceive to be their true sense of self. This is not about privileging the self at the expense of all other people, as is often the implicit suggestion behind a lot of narcissistic personal development literature. Rather, it is about finding ways for families to co-exist in genuine mutuality that does not involve unsustainable sacrifice, rather fruitful exchange.

6: ARCHETYPES

The Conspiracy

So far we have looked at how several key themes—history, sexuality, relationships, and fatherhood—are mobilized by the conspiracy in society at large to promote a specific and prescriptive vision of masculinity that bears little witness to the diversity of men's experiences. In this chapter we will look at how archetypes have been used as a way of understanding masculinity within the context of men's movement literature that began gaining momentum in the early 1990s, and which has continuing influence today.

An archetype is a template that can be used to describe various universal themes and motifs, most commonly employed in myths. The psychologist Carl Jung used archetypes as a way of understanding particular models of human behavior and characteristics, the basis of which can be discovered deep in the human psyche, and is shared across people and cultures. To be sure, this is a very simplistic description of Jung's understanding of archetypes, which was both complex and dependent on the stages of his own conceptual development. However, the way the men's movement uses Jungian archetypes is equally simplistic, so it will suffice for our discussion, at least as we allow the conspiracy to talk in its own voice in the first section, *The Conspiracy*. We'll tentatively scratch the surface of what else resides behind the concept of archetypes in the following sections, the analytical *The Problem*, and the more visionary *The Solution*.

The two books examined in this chapter are themselves archetypal of men's movement literature, or a particular type of men's movement called the mythopoetic men's movement, which made use of myth, metaphor and story to understand models for masculinity. The mythopoetic men's movement is most notably connected with the poet Robert Bly, and we will look at his 1990 book *Iron John: A Book About Men*. Bly's book started a movement that garnered significant media attention at the time with stories about men's groups taking place in the woods, where partially-clothed and bearded men would get in touch with their "inner," "mature," or "deep" masculinity. Shortly after this came our second book, *King, Warrior, Magician, Lover: Rediscovering the Archetypes of the Mature Masculine* by Robert Moore and Douglas Gillette. These two books catalyzed a large volume of literature that, while less read today within the context of the men's movement, is still influential in the way various forms of personal development coaches, popular psychologists and spiritual gurus describe masculinity.

Bly's book, *Iron John*, recreates a Grimm Brothers tale about a young boy who meets a wild hairy man—Iron John—who becomes the boy's mentor and leads him through various stages of development via initiation into maturity. Bly's main point is that contemporary men have become "soft" and disconnected from their inner wildness. Men have been disempowered in culture, television, literature, and are too often presented as bumbling fools: "When we walk into a contemporary house," writes Bly, "it is often the mother who comes forward confidently. The father is somewhere else in the back, being inarticulate."

A significant part of the problem identified by Bly is the nature of modern work, which since the Industrial Revolution has removed men ever further from their families, in particular their sons. This has prevented them from bonding with their sons and initiating them into manhood: as such, we have a whole society that has never entered full initiated maturity. The result is what Bly describes as the "sibling society," in which immature men are suspicious of older men and authority, while at the same time being naïve about men their own age and women in general. The absence of sufficient father-son relationships is also described by Bly as the "father wound," which we touched upon briefly in the previous chapter about fatherhood.

Bly claims that contemporary men can counter this problem by rediscovering the Wild Man (Iron John) within. While the Wild Man is a psychological archetype, Bly also extends the metaphor to include wildness in nature, where he believes masculinity most naturally resides: "to receive initiation truly means to expand sideways into the glory of oaks, mountains, glaciers, horses, lions, grasses, waterfalls, deer. We need wilderness and extravagance. Whatever shuts a human being away from the waterfall and the tiger will kill him," writes Bly, citing Francis of Assisi and Henry David Thoreau as two "nature mystics" who appropriately communed with the land and exuded wildness. Bly believes there is a uniqueness to masculinity which, while also accessible to women, is rendered most eloquently in men: "in the man's heart there is a low string that makes his whole chest tremble when the qualities of the masculine are spoken of in the right way."

It is important to remember that while the mythopoetic men's movement was often perceived as the "spiritual men's movement," it is chiefly psychological: Bly claims archetypes dwell "at the bottom of [the] psyche," among "other interior beings," which runs counter to a commonly-held assumption that archetypes are spiritual in character. We will explore the nature of masculine spirituality in the next chapter, but it's useful to note that Bly is curiously hostile to the spiritual in *Iron John*, basing much of his critique on re-asserting the masculine (in the stereotypical understand of the word). Bly prefers Old Testament Christianity, paganism and indigenous spirituality to contemporary or orthodox religious observance, which he perceives as being insufficiently masculine and wild.

The psychological and even biological basis for archetypes is more explicitly articulated by Robert Moore and Douglas Gillette in *King, Warrior, Magician, Lover*. They describe archetypes as being "hard wired" in the reptilian brain. While Bly focuses on the Wild Man archetype, Moore and Gillette focus on the King and Warrior (all four archetypes referred to in their book title are explored, but it is notable that the Magician and Lover—which resonate far less with stereotypical and combative models of masculinity—have gained far less attention in the men's movement).

Moore and Gillette claim the King archetype "is primal in all men" and "comes first in importance." The King is based on creative principles, inasmuch as he literally creates the world (his kingdom) around him. To the individuals who reject the King's world he says, "you are chaos, demonic," and more than this, "you are noncreation, nonworld." The King, then, is a reality-defining entity who Moore and Gillette intend to be of a generative or benign nature: his leadership principles are similar to the model of servant leadership discussed in the previous Fatherhood chapter (the father, if you like, is a domestic King archetype). There is a definite majesty behind the King archetype—and thus in masculinity—in every sense of the word: Moore and Gillette describe its return in our barren contemporary culture as an, "intuition of holiness … both dreadful and wonderful by virtue of its power … It drops us to our knees with the force of its holiness." Should readers require music to help evoke this Kingly drama, Moore and Gillette direct them towards, "soundtracks from 'sword and sandals' movies like *Spartacus* or *Ben Hur*."

Just as the King is inherent in the male psyche (indeed, of primary importance within it), so too the Warrior archetype, which Moore and Gillette identify in numerous domains, both natural and fictitious. Moore and Gillette appeal to the great apes to explain what they perceive to be the natural basis for the Warrior archetype. They cite Jane Goodall's study of chimpanzees, who initially were thought to be peaceful but ended up being Warrior-like (brutal), the suggestion being if the chimpanzees cannot remain peaceful, how can men? (You may remember how the appeal to the animal kingdom was discussed back in the History chapter.) They go on to argue, "What accounts for the popularity of Rambo, or Arnold Schwarzenegger, of war movies like *Apocalypse Now*, *Platoon*, *Full Metal Jacket* and many, many more? We can deplore the violence in these movies, as well as on our television screens, but, obviously, the Warrior still remains very much alive in us." The prevalence of violence, both in the human and animal kingdom, is seen as evidence for the natural and rightful role of the Warrior as a defining characteristic of masculinity.

Further positively-framed examples of the Warrior include the shifting tactics of fencers and guerrilla soldiers, and the split-second decision making of "a good Marine." Just as readers seeking to evoke the King archetype are directed towards "swords and sandals" cinematic references, for the Warrior Moore and Gillette suggest inspiration can be found with the exemplar of Yul Brynner in *The Magnificent Seven* who, "says little, moves with the physical control of a predator, attacks only the enemy and has absolute mastery over the technology of his trade." Moore and Gillette even co-opt religiosity into their search for the universal Warrior, citing Jesus and Buddha (as they both had to endure temptation) and Islam which, "as a whole is built on Warrior energy" (one wonders if this would have been so enthusiastically employed in a post-9/11 world).

There is a stylistic and structural element to Moore and Gillette's presentation of archetypes that also appeals to a commonly accepted (in other words, conspiratorial) model of masculinity. Their introduction states, "our purpose in writing this book … has been to offer men a simplified and readable outline of an 'operator's manual for the male psyche.' Reading this book should help you understand your strengths and weaknesses as a man and provide you with a map to the territories of masculine selfhood which you still need to explore." The Mars-like masculine characteristics suggested by John Gray in the Relationships chapter are evident here: the "operator's manual," and the "map to the territories." Moore and Gillette divide their archetypal map up into four quadrants, which offers a model suggesting some kind of systematic or scientific rigor, and which shares a commonality with Ken Wilber's map of the human psyche, as referred to in the History chapter.

The four quadrants do not just map out different types of archetypes, but balance elements both within and between archetypes. Moore and Gillette aim to be cautious, reminding us that archetypes need to be offset by other archetypes to produce full and rich personalities. For example, the Warrior might be offset with the lover to produce depth and nobility to what might otherwise be a rather mono-dimensional "real" person (Winston Churchill, Yukio Mishima and General Patton are referred to in regard to this particular combination: make of that what you will). The balancing element is also addressed with the notion of the "shadow," which is when an individual over-identifies with an archetype, or has mobilized archetypal energies in negative ways due to insufficiently addressed neuroses or character flaws.

In sum, there are very clear messages to be had about masculinity and archetypes from Bly, Moore and Gillette:

- Archetypes are inescapable character templates that are rooted either in the depths of the human psyche or the reptilian brain.

- Masculinity is defined by a particular set of archetypes: namely the Wild Man, King and Warrior (echoing those repeated themes of masculinity being about aggression, assertiveness, leadership and the public domain).

- Modern society is out of touch with these archetypal energies and must re-connect with them via a process of initiation to solve our social ills.

- Masculine archetypes must be combined or balanced with other archetypes in order not to manifest the "shadow" or negative character traits.

The Problem

I've written about the problem with archetypes in a detailed (read academic) fashion in my earlier book, *Numen, Old Men: Contemporary Masculine Spiritualities and the Problem of Patriarchy*. A good deal from this section (and in some other chapters) is drawn from that book: I'm telling you this so if you happen to have read it you won't feel deceived about repeated content, and also so that you don't *have* to go and read it, or know where to look for greater depth on the subject.

The mythopoetic men's movement made a great deal about its use of "Jungian" archetypes, suggesting it was drawing upon a deep and sophisticated psychological and analytical heritage. The reality is somewhat different, which has resulted in the movement more accurately being described as "neo-Jungian," which in more everyday language might be translated as "Jung lite." There isn't the space here to outline how the mythopoetic men's movement misread Jung, but suffice to say Jungian scholar David Tacey has charged it with "conservative and simplistic appropriation of Jungian theory." The archetypes the movement aspires to are, in short, simply reflections of the way masculinity is modeled within the conspiracy or, as masculinities researcher and counselor Philip Culbertson has described them, such archetypes are "calcifications of a patriarchal world view." What I'm more interested in are the types of masculinity such archetypes promote and some of the more general problems with identifying with archetypes (in a neo-Jungian, if not genuinely Jungian sense).

Take, for example, the Wild Man. Let us put aside the problematic issue about initiation around which the *Iron John* story revolves, as I have shown how this is a conformist strategy on behalf of the conspiracy in the previous Fatherhood chapter. It is a simple fact that Bly claims wildness is the essence of masculinity: it is a clear and prescriptive statement. If you have no inclinations to wildness, in all its earthiness and hairiness, Bly believes you are missing the essence of masculinity and are presumably one of the "soft males" he identifies on numerous occasions in *Iron John*.

Bly suggests, with his allusion to "the glory of oaks, mountains, glaciers, horses, lions, grasses, waterfalls, deer," that there is something inherently beautiful about wildness, as if the psychic wildness of masculinity is the same thing as the majestic wildness of nature. But this is not so: the psychic wildness that Bly refers to is subject to all the pathologies and neuroses instilled by the conspiracy, whereas nature is not (although nature is massively impacted by the dominating mindset of the conspiracy, but that's another story).

Folklorist Jack Zipes does a great job of teasing out some of the inherent messages of *Iron John* and the Grimm Brothers tale, *Iron Hans*, on which it is based. In its original form, the Wild Man folklore archetype was a demonic figure, not a mentor. Further still, the tale was used not to encourage some "natural" masculine wildness, but to initiate young aristocrats into the role of warrior or king. Zipes concludes that, "both *Iron Hans* and *Iron John* are *warrior* tales, and both celebrate violence and killing as the means to establish male identity." Is that the kind of masculinity we really want? Certainly not, but it's the kind of masculinity the conspiracy promotes, as we have seen specifically in the History chapter.

And of course, one does not need to look to the pre-history of mythopoetic men's movement literature to see this pre-occupation with violence, as Moore and Gillette's book indicates. As I mentioned before, Moore and Gillette deal equally with the four archetypes of King, Warrior, Magician and Lover. However, when the book was first written, far more attention was given to the conspiratorially-flavored King and Warrior archetypes than to the Magician and Lover. Two decades later, mobilization of the Warrior archetype *by far* outstrips all other archetypes and can be found in a range of men's movement contexts such as The ManKind Project, counseling and group work, and a range of alternative spiritualities, whether of an earthy nature (such as Paganism) or corporate nature (such as Integral Spirituality).

Moore and Gillette's presentation of the warrior archetype would be funny were it not intended so seriously, and it is no surprise that such literature was lampooned at the time by satirists such as Alfred Gingold and his book *Fire in the John: The Manly Man in the Age of Sissification*. The appeal to swords and sandals movie soundtracks and Yul Brynner genuinely make it appear as if they are playing for laughs, but it is a tragedy rather than a comedy, because so many men continue to take them seriously by appealing to the "warrior within."

I find it deeply disturbing that questions such as, "What accounts for the popularity of Rambo, or Arnold Schwarzenegger, of war movies like *Apocalypse Now*, *Platoon*, *Full Metal Jacket* and many, many more?" can be answered with the assumption that the warrior archetype is natural in all of us. At the very least, equal consideration must be given to the answer that we have been systemically conditioned into violence by the conspiracy. Indeed, it seems like something of a conspiratorial cover-up that such a question is not given adequate consideration by writers with otherwise serious and clever backgrounds.

This is the way the conspiracy works: the blindingly obvious is routinely overlooked and replaced with what, on examination, are quite absurd suggestions that are commonly accepted as true.

As I reiterate repeatedly throughout this text, *when something appears to be natural, we are often witnessing the conspiracy conditioning our understanding of how masculinity is defined.* In the current context, there is plenty of awareness that the warrior is a problematic model to follow, as demonstrated by the need to routinely qualify it by such terms as "peaceful warrior" or "noble warrior." But warriors are what warriors do, and that is facilitating violence and death. But such is the effective conditioning of the conspiracy, that even those who identify a problem would rather soften or sanitize the concept of the warrior than reject it out of hand, which is by far the most sensible thing to do.

What this qualification also suggests is that the task at hand for an individual is to identify with the "spirit" or "essence" of an archetype rather than fully embodying it, which can lead to problems, or what is referred to as the "shadow" of the archetype. However, there are no effective strategies provided for how to achieve this, and knowing when enough is enough: it relies on individuals knowing what is "wrong" and what sensibly resides in the "shadow." However, given that everyone has different values, and even smart writers such as Moore and Gillette do not ask necessary and blindingly obvious questions about why things are the way they are, such "knowing" is rife with danger.

Let's have a look in a bit of detail at how such a process is insufficiently addressed. The following example from Moore and Gillette discusses the Shadow King, which should be the ideal opportunity to nail down the problematic nature of both Kingship and navigating the shadow:

> In the story of King David and Bathsheba, Bathsheba was the wife of another man, Uriah the Hittite. One day David was walking on the roof of his palace when he spotted Bathsheba bathing. He was so aroused by this sight that he sent for her and forced her to have sex with him. In theory, remember, all the women of the realm were the king's. But they belonged to the *archetype* of the king, not to the mortal king. David unconsciously identified himself with the King energy and not only took

Bathsheba but also had her husband, Uriah, killed. Fortunately for the kingdom, David had a conscience in the form of Nathan the prophet, who came to him and indicted him. David, much to his credit, accepted the truth of the indictment and repented.

Moore and Gillette's point is that if a man identifies with the shadow aspect of the King archetype he will become tyrannical. They state that, "as is the case with all archetypes, the King displays an active-passive bipolar shadow structure," yet their example of such shows David identifying not with the shadow but the *archetype itself*: "David unconsciously identified himself with the King energy." The shadow is the net effect of the identification, not part of "an active-passive bipolar shadow structure." This represents one of the least practical elements in the whole mythopoetic call to archetypes: identify with the archetype to find your wholeness, but do not identify too much. One must wonder that if King David found this process tricky, with all his experience navigating kingly energy, what hope is there for the average man? Let us give Moore and Gillette the benefit of the doubt on this confusion.

Moore and Gillette say, "In theory, remember, all the women of the realm were the king's." "But," say Moore and Gillette, anticipating the feminist outcry, "they belonged to the *archetype* of the king, not to the mortal king." One must therefore assume that belonging to an archetypal dominating structure is considered less oppressive than a real one. "David unconsciously identified himself with the King energy and not only took Bathsheba but also had her husband, Uriah, killed." In short, by being a rapist and a murderer David bears witness to King energy, not just in its shadow form, but its full archetypal form. "Fortunately for the kingdom, David had a conscience in the form of Nathan the prophet, who came to him and indicted him." In other words, David did not have a personal conscience, rather an external conscience which was enforced upon him in the same way that fairness must be enforced upon all conspiratorial models of power, for it does not eventuate of its own accord. Even then, David is removed from the equation, as the indictment is not fortunate for David personally (though one assumes he had some desire to redeem himself before God) but "the kingdom." "David, much to his credit, accepted the truth of the indictment and repented." So, King David is an archetypal-delusional murdering rapist who requires external pressure to awaken his conscience for the sake of the supposed greater good, but "much to his credit" he repents. It is as if Moore and Gillette have unconsciously identified *themselves* with David and are in need of their own prophet Nathan to point out the deeply disturbing nature of the King. At best the King is a benevolent dictator, at worst a despot.

So the conspiracy mobilizes archetypes in a very specific way: it suggests there is a narrow range of characteristics that are "natural" to masculinity: it allows very little diversity, suggesting anything which falls outside these characteristics is insufficiently masculine or, in Bly's words, "soft." Note another strategy here: the lip service to a broader range or archetypes and balance. Certainly, both Bly and Moore and Gillette refer to a broader range of archetypes than those that are overtly dominating and combative. Certainly, both Bly and Moore and Gillette refer to the danger of identifying with the shadow aspect of archetypes and the pathologies that can result. This allows them to have their cake and eat it. When people like me come along and point out the problematic nature of pathological kings and warriors, they point to the other archetypes as evidence that the criticism is selective, yet their massive weighting towards kings and warriors is itself selective, and it is deceptive to suggest that alternative archetypes are given equal consideration.

At the end of the day, these writers know that if they want to sell books and get bums on seats at workshops they have to appeal to a populist understanding of masculinity, which until the conspiracy is overturned at a systemic level can only ever mirror the conspiracy. I suspect that a lot of writers who appear to support the conspiracy do so not because they firmly believe in what they are writing, but because *they know there is a market* for what they are writing, and because they enjoy the privileged position of being a thought leader within that market. Speaking out against the conspiracy is, after all, a lonely place to be, and certainly does not pay the rent (we'll explore the financial motivation behind the conspiracy in more depth in the concluding chapter).

So to recap, there are various problems with the way the mythopoetic men's movement uses archetypes as models for masculinity:

- The archetypes used have none of the subtlety or nuance intended by Jung, rather reflecting commonly held, conspiratorial perceptions of masculinity.

- Those perceptions of masculinity are largely pathological: the violence of being a Wild Man or Warrior, or the domination of being a King.

- There is no adequate system in place to explain how men should identify with the archetype, but not so much that they inhabit its "shadow" aspect.

- References to a broader range or archetypes and the "shadow" give the impression of balance, but this is at best lip service to balance or at worse deception.

The Solution

There are three key strategies for mitigating the problems caused by the men's movement and their use of archetypes. The first strategy, and one that I find most compelling, is to simply reject them out of hand. I can appreciate that Jung may have had subtler intentions about archetypes, and that today it is also possible to imagine different types of archetypes. However, my feeling is the common understanding of archetypes is ingrained in such a problematic way in popular culture that those more useful levels of meaning will forever be eclipsed, and it is best to redeploy that meaning in an altogether different type of language.

The problem, though, is that because archetypes—as a *metaphor for understanding reality*, rather than a psychic reality in themselves—are so deeply ingrained in society, it seems almost impossible for people to shake free of them. As such, we are left with strategies two and three: creating *different types* of archetypes and *thinking differently about the nature* of archetypes.

As I mentioned above, while greatest attention was given to Moore and Gillette's King and Warrior archetypes, they also wrote about the Magician and Lover. In a similar way, while Bly wrote chiefly of the Wild Man, he also referred to other archetypes (albeit not in any productive manner) such as the Mythologist or Cook and Grief Man. Back at the height of the mythopoetic years, some effort was made to redress this balance. For example, Glenn Mazis wrote a book called, *The Trickster, Magician and Grieving Man*, but it sank largely without trace because its rejection of the hero motif ran counter to the kind of conspiratorial masculine fantasies found elsewhere in the movement.

In a similar way, Aaron Kipnis wrote approvingly of the Green Man as an archetype, a largely pagan understanding of masculinity that combined it with the more nurturing and organic characteristics of what is commonly perceived of as the Earth Mother. Kipnis' Green Man—described as "a creative, fecund, nurturing, protective, and compassionate male, existing in harmony with the earth and the feminine, yet also erotic, free, wild, playful, energetic, and fierce"—is useful in trying to offer different archetypes, but also shows how difficult it is to erase conspiratorial themes. For example, these counter-conspiratorial characteristics are muted when Kipnis goes on to remind readers that Green Man energy also envelopes carving a phallic staff, copulating on the 30-foot-long penis of the Cerne Giant and having the power of massive erect trees. The reader is stirred in the knowledge that he can be simultaneously nurturing *and* hard, in every way: with the Green Man, just as with the rest of the conspiracy, the cock is always central.

But there remains, nonetheless, some benefit to this line of thought. The Trickster archetype is, I believe, particularly useful. It has the potential to offer a framework for masculine characteristics that may or may not be stereotypical. Importantly, too, its values range from playful through to malicious. The Trickster always resides in shades of gray—rather than being black or white—which, as an analogy, is more representative of the truth when looking for models for masculinities. For those who find the Trickster too akin to a medieval joker or Castaneda-like, I would suggest a more contemporary version of the Hacker. The Hacker archetype again may or may not be stereotypically masculine: he may be imagined as an epic battler with his acts of online transgression, but equally can be a scrawny loser living with his parents. A spectrum of values is also apparent: white hat hackers who are there to transparently highlight flaws in data security; black hat hackers who are overtly villainous and out for personal gain; and that vast section in the middle, the gray hat hacker who, like most real people, comprises a bit of everything. I certainly see myself as a gray hat type.

One other useful archetype that may be worth considering is drawn from gay literature, the Androgyne. Toby Johnson writes of the Androgyne, "a potent blending of male strength and competence and of female sensitivity and feeling makes for a more interesting human being with a more complex and fascinating personality." It's interesting to note that while the Androgyne is discussed here within the context of gayness, there is nothing about it that requires same-sex attraction: any straight man should be able to embody the Androgyne without compromising even his commonly-understood sexuality (let a lone a more fluid version of the same, as suggested in the Sexuality chapter).

There is, however, a word of caution in regard to the Androgyne, which is useful to remember whenever the idea of "balance" is tabled. Johnson's reference to "male strength and competence" and "female sensitivity and feeling" might initially look like a good idea, but those images of male and female are drawn directly from the conspiracy. A more useful way of thinking about the Androgyne would be to unhook "male" from "strength and competence" and "female" from "sensitivity and feeling" and allow those characteristics to reside side-by-side without any connection to biological sex. The Androgyne is then not a combination of conspiratorial masculine and feminine, but a separate category altogether, and one which itself is not a fixed, prescribed archetype, rather a broad spectrum of positions. We are not looking for a "third gender" here: we are looking for multiple alternatives to the conspiratorial binary understanding of gender.

This separate category altogether, one which itself is not a fixed, prescribed archetype, rather a broad spectrum of positions, is an ideal segue from our two strategies of thinking about *different types* of archetypes to thinking *differently about* archetypes. To begin with, as I have already noted, the mythopoetic understanding of archetypes is a greatly simplified version of Jung's presentation of archetypes. A vast volume of words could be consumed discussing what Jung did and did not mean, but suffice to say he was a product of his time and cannot be taken as an exemplar for how people should be thinking about gender in the present day.

Of significant interest is the 2009 publication of Jung's visionary journal *The Red Book*, the editor of which—Sonu Shamdasani—claims is "nothing less than the central book in his oeuvre," and that his other work cannot really be understood without reading this in tandem. There is little in *The Red Book* that resonates with a mythopoetic understanding of masculinity, and it would be interesting to speculate how the mythopoetic movement would have been different if it had this source at its disposal. Remember, too, that Jung was at heart a mythologist: he constructed ways of understanding reality *through* and *as* myth. The mythopoetic movement repeatedly referred to story and myth, and repeatedly conflated it with reality: for archetypes to be useful they must *genuinely* be considered mythical, with all the caveats that implies.

Further still, however much we unpack what Jung may or may not have understood by archetypes, his is not the only view on the matter. As one commenter (Butters) on the first online chapter of *The Masculinity Conspiracy* writes:

> I hope your definition of archetypes do not rest on one definition of them only—the classical Jungian definition. The Archetypal Psychology school of thought, which branched from Jung in the work of James Hillman, and was popularized by Thomas Moore (e.g. *Care of the Soul*) is at least as popular as the classical definition of archetypes. Difference being that the classical school perpetuates stereotypes under the name archetypes, whereas the movement launched by Hillman and co has philosophically corrected the limitations of the former. The Archetypal Psychology branch of Jung's Analytical psychology is almost completely compatible with the notion of a plurality of masculinities and indeed promotes the cause very strongly among the masses! For instance, Hillman and co state that both sexes have equal access to roles of nurturer (Geb/Gaia), the Warrior (Athena/Ares), the lover of beauty (Adonis/Aphrodite), the power/status seekers (Zeus/Hera).

I don't cite Butters here to agree with him (I'm not sufficiently informed on archetypal psychology to have a useful opinion), rather to demonstrate that there are always different takes on such things, many of which get overlooked by the popular discourse on the subject at hand.

I believe the simplest way to usefully mobilize archetypes is to think of them not as *models* for (in our case) masculinity, rather as *elements* of self (which may or may not be gendered). For example, I'll list some elements that first spring to mind when I describe myself (in no specific order): writer, thinker, father, husband, loner, son, neurotic, visionary, polemicist, contrarian. All these words describe elements that go towards the construction of my complete sense of self, but no single one gets anywhere near that complete sense of self. Indeed, to pick any single word almost immediately suggests a narrow perception of self that borders on pathological.

Thinking archetypically in a useful way would therefore involve identifying a range of individual elements and fashioning from them a sufficiently nuanced sense of self. Some of these elements (such as father, husband, son) may have a clear connection with biological sex; most will not. *Any archetypal element that is not based in biological sex is socially constructed and therefore open to all people, male or female.* The conspiracy works by reducing the number of elements available to a person to a very low number (say, one to four elements), and then—in practice—assigning those elements exclusively to either men or women. To counter the conspiracy we make any number of elements available to the individual and allow them to be assigned to any individual, in any way the individual sees fit (this is not about prescribing values, after all, rather enabling possibilities, which may not always be pleasant).

The result is an "elemental suite" or an "archetypal suite" that is bound by nothing other than the individual's values, characteristics and desires. It is unlikely that a sufficiently nuanced suite could be described as either masculine or feminine. But, importantly, this does not reduce the suite to being "gender-neutral" (as Mansfield would have argued in the History chapter). Instead, the suite is "gender unique," each one bearing witness to the specific way the individual navigates their complex journey between biological sex, the expectations of a prescriptive conspiratorial model of gender, and aspirations for freedom from that conspiratorial model.

Importantly, some of those suites may look identical to a conspiratorial understanding of gender, as genuine freedom must allow for any particular combination. The big difference is that in the model I am suggesting, the suite that resembles the conspiracy is achieved via a proactive choice to construct that suite, not because it is "natural" or "appropriate." This is the fundamental difference between my message and the message you will read in most popular books about masculinity. When I critique conspiratorial models of masculinity, I am not *denying* those models (although I *am* showing how they are problematic);

rather, I am denying the conspiratorial claim about what masculinity *should be*, and offering not a specific alternative but the freedom to choose.

7: SPIRITUALITY

The Conspiracy

In our allegedly increasingly secular age it is tempting to think that spirituality is a rather niche subject to explore in regard to the masculinity conspiracy, but this couldn't be further from the truth. To begin with, a number of the writers we have met in the preceding chapters have intersected with spirituality. In the History chapter, Ken Wilber's worldview is dominated by a developmental–spiritual framework. In the Sexuality chapter, both David Deida and Robert Lawlor have what might be called a "cosmological"—if not explicitly spiritual—outlook on life. In the Relationships chapter, John Gray's work is informed by his years as a monk and assistant to Maharishi Mahesh Yogi, founder of Transcendental Meditation. In the Fatherhood chapter, Stephen James, David Thomas and Rick Johnson all have a Christian background. And in the previous chapter, while I have argued that archetypes are largely of a psychological rather than spiritual nature, the mythopoetic movement is commonly understood as the "spiritual men's movement."

Certainly, if I had selected the conspiracy texts differently, this "spiritual" aspect might have been less pronounced, but it nevertheless demonstrates that spirituality still has a profound impact upon modern life in general, and the conspiracy in particular. This fact is even becoming amplified as our understanding of the term "spirituality" evolves. A generation ago, spirituality had clear connotations of a relationship with a supernatural or creative principal in the universe. Today we are witnessing what is described as the "subjective turn" in which people turn away from external sources of authority (such as the church) and look instead inwards to their personal "values" as the defining site of their spiritual experience. This means that a lot of people are interpreting anything that involves contemplation and an exploration of their interiority as "spiritual" (typified by the *Eat Pray Love* phenomenon). I would argue this both dilutes the nature of spirituality and denies fruitful atheistic philosophical endeavors, but that's another story. The point being, *spirituality is everywhere.*

As with all chapters, my selection of two conspiratorial texts excludes so many important points of discussion. I've chosen first *No More Christian Nice Guy: When Being Nice—Instead of Good—Hurts Men, Women and Children* by Paul Coughlin. This book is a good example of the Christian preoccupation with masculinity that has been bubbling away since the Muscular Christianity movement of the 1850s, and which shares many concerns with contemporary spiritualities that are not connected with any particular spiritual tradition. Clearly, such an evangelical Christian text glosses over the many important distinctions that could be made not just within different Christian denominations but also different faith traditions. Second, I've chosen *The Hidden Spirituality of Men: Ten Metaphors to Awaken the Sacred Masculine* by Matthew Fox. The selection of this text serves three functions: it speaks to a spirituality less grounded in an orthodox tradition; it picks up the themes of archetypes from the previous chapter; it shows how even writers who intend to seek different forms of masculinity can get caught in the conspiratorial trap.

Paul Coughlin's *No More Christian Nice Guy* relies heavily on the work of Robert Glover, a psychotherapist who identified the so-called "Nice Guy Syndrome" where men are said to suppress their own needs by seeking the constant approval of others. Coughlin's task has been to map the Nice Guy Syndrome on to his experiences of the church. Coughlin's main argument is that Christian men are being sold an incorrect image of Jesus as a nice guy when in fact He was not *nice*, but *good* in a proactive fashion. Consequently Coughlin identifies, "passive naïve Christian Nice Guys. We sit next to them in church all the time, not realizing their identity is being squashed, their will being broken." "Valorous niceness," says Coughlin, "is often cowardly passivity in disguise."

Coughlin sees the typical Christian Nice Guy rendering of Jesus as a "bearded woman" as part of "woman worship: the domestic cult," which shares a distinct similarity with Robert Bly's comment about, "When we walk into a contemporary house, it is often the mother who comes forward confidently. The father is somewhere else in the back, being inarticulate." Coughlin believes that men have been domesticated and that home life has become the exclusive domain of women. Indeed, he sees this as part of larger program of what he perceives to be "America's feminized faith." In Coughlin's view, men need to toughen up in the home and in the church, and bring both back into line with more authentic Christ-like masculine values. Men need to assert their God-given masculinity. The typical form of Christian meek masculinity that Coughlin bemoans is what keeps men away from the church. He argues: "When we're free from the myths that Jesus is the Supreme Nice Guy, that the Father is the cosmic teddy bear, and that the Holy Spirit is a docile, breezy presence, men will find the church more compelling and relevant."

Consequently, asserting God-given masculinity is about rediscovering the real Jesus who, far from being passive, was very assertive. When opening up to the real Jesus, Coughlin highlights the following words and phrases that describe the tough Christly context Christian men should keep in mind when their faith suggests they be nice: "shouting, wilderness, sins, camel hair, locusts, slave, split open, tempted, Satan, arrested, the time has come!, possessed, evil spirit, destroy, be quiet!, screamed, convulsed, amazement, high fever, victims, alone, leprosy, begging, moved with pity, be healed!, examine, secluded." Counter to the passive Christian masculinity Coughlin sees around him, he reminds readers that, "the gospel includes dirty feet, stinky hair, fish guts, bugs between the teeth, dirt under it's nails ... smell the adrenaline, feel your heart pound, taste the locust that lingers on your lips." In short, Jesus righteously kicked ass—hard and often—which is what Christian men should be doing to embody their Christ-like masculinity.

But short of defining masculinity as whatever Jesus and other divinely-inspired Biblical men did, what does Coughlin actually mean by masculinity? Coughlin looks to the 1905 edition of *Webster's* for answers: "virile, not feminine or effeminate; strong; robust." It is also singular and particular in nature: he refers to "real men" and "true masculinity." In the "masculinity defined" section Coughlin writes that "Biblical masculinity is guys doing what God wants guys to do, and doing it in line with their true identity—before it was marred by human sin and especially shame—leading to a virtuous life marked by redemptive creativity, protection, purpose, and love." Further still we are told that "masculinity is spelled p-r-o-a-c-t-i-v-e ... Accept these facts: Life is a difficult battle, demanding conflict and struggle ... *You'll make much more progress when you're offensive*" (original emphasis). Christian men, writes Coughlin, should "embrace Christ's tough, courageous, protective, assertive personality, which invigorates real male sensibilities."

In *The Hidden Spirituality of Men* Matthew Fox presents a different form of masculine spirituality. While Fox was for many years a Catholic priest, his flavor of spirituality is not bound to any particular tradition, drawing equally on Buddhism and Judaism, as well as indigenous and pagan spiritualities. For Fox, the spirituality of men is hidden largely due to self-preservation. Society expects certain things from men, and anything that does not align with those expectations must be hidden and silenced.

Spirituality, so often perceived as feminine, is one such element that men must hide and silence, both from other men and women, and even themselves.

But, contrary to Coughlin, Fox does not seek solely a conspiratorial vision of masculinity, in other words that assertive, go-getting combative manliness based on a militaristic vision of Christ. Instead he seeks ten "metaphors" for men to follow, by which he really means ten archetypes. The shifting of language from *archetypes* to *metaphors* is a signal that Fox is aware of the pitfalls of archetypal thinking, as outlined in the previous chapter. Indeed, he rightly critiques Robert Moore and Douglas Gillette's use of archetypes as "bent on defining masculinity in a crazy macho way." Fox is keen to point out the dangers of taking archetypes too literally, and connecting the "gender" of the archetype with actual gender. Instead, he sees the archetypes as "ten stories, ten images, ten ways that men and boys, women and girls can relate to the masculine inside themselves" rather than something men should specifically aspire to as a way of manifesting their masculinity. Fox is also aware of the problems of Christian masculinity, taking care to highlight the problems of Promise Keepers (who promote servant leadership, which I discussed in the Fatherhood chapter).

The ten archetypes of authentic masculinity of which Fox writes are: Father Sky; the Green Man; Icarus and Daedalus; Hunter-Gatherers; Spiritual Warriors; Masculine Sexuality, Numinous Sexuality; Cosmic and Animal Bodies; the Blue Man; Earth Father; Grandfather Sky. Father Sky refers to a range of ancient and contemporary "sky gods" which offer men metaphors for a masculine framing of the spiritual. The Green Man provides a masculine earthly complement to Father Sky (and Mother Earth), connecting men to the earth and providing an ecological consciousness more typical of feminist and women's spiritualities. Icarus and Daedalus speaks to communication between the generations, either between father and son, or more generally in society which often undervalues the passion of youth while over-valuing the wisdom of elders.

Hunter-Gatherers resonates with men's historical and contemporary desire to engage with this activity, the need for ritual, individual and collective intelligence, and the ability to appropriately address shame and anger. Spiritual Warriors find appropriate ways for men to channel aggression with nobility rather than mindless militarism. Masculine Sexuality, Numinous Sexuality is concerned with bridging the gap between spirituality and sexuality and also between gay and straight men. Cosmic and Animal Bodies refers to a celebration rather than denial of the body within spiritual pursuits. The Blue Man resonates with an expansion of masculine spiritual consciousness, compassion and creativity. The Earth Father calls for a more generative and caring model of paternalism directed towards the whole community as well as our own children. Grandfather Sky is a metaphor for how older men are of value, of how they can both guide and learn from younger people.

After dealing with these metaphors, Fox offers a treatment of what he describes as "sacred marriages" which deals largely with the theme of complementarity and the union between masculine and feminine. Fox also expands sacred marriage to include other types of union: between dualism and non-dualism, East and West, humanity and the Divine, ecumenism, lay and monastic practices, indigenous and postmodern ceremonies, left- and right-brain thinking, gay and straight orientations, young and old. Fox's particular use of archetypes certainly elevates them out of the purely psychological domain of those discussed in the previous chapter, and clearly calls for a more diverse and balanced understanding of masculinity. But, as we shall see in the following section, they still perpetuate the conspiracy.

In sum, the conspiracy mobilizes spirituality by presenting masculinity in specific ways, within both a traditional faith context such as Christianity, or a contemporary spirituality that both draws upon and transcends such traditional faiths. In particular:

- Christianity is presented as being a "feminized" faith that needs to reclaim its authentic masculine essence.

- Christian men need to become more masculine by modeling themselves not on an effeminate and meek portrayal of Jesus, but a wilder, angrier Jesus.

- Christian masculinity is about being virile, proactive and on the offensive.

- More generally, masculine spirituality may be thought of in relation to specific metaphors or archetypes.

- Masculine spirituality should be kept in balance and thought of in terms of complementarity with feminine spirituality, or a "sacred marriage."

The Problem

It doesn't take much examination to discover that the foundations upon which Christian masculinity bases its concerns are rather shaky. The concern is that men are disappearing from the church as a result of rampant feminization, and that the church therefore needs to man-up to get back to masculine basics. The reality is that yes, men are underrepresented in church attendance (statistics of congregations being two-thirds women are commonly quoted). But a quick look at who *runs* the church (including even the most progressive of denominations) shows a *massive* weighting towards male leadership.

Also, it seems a rather selective approach to history to claim the feminization thesis, as some of the identifying aspects of the Christian era such as monasticism and mission have a very masculine flavor. It is interesting to note, too, that those forms of Christianity that buck today's trend and flourish tend to be those which resonate more with conspiratorial models of masculinity (evangelicalism in the United States with its appeal to servant leadership, and conservative Anglicanism in Nigeria with its homophobia, for example). What we are witnessing is not a feminization of the church, rather an overwhelmingly masculine church responding anxiously to an increasingly vocal opposition that demands justice and questions the conspiratorial grip of masculine power (at a systemic if not personal level).

However, this doesn't speak specifically to the kinds of masculinity promoted in the conspiratorial texts at hand. Coughlin wants men to be inspired by a tougher vision of Jesus, rather than that of a "bearded woman." The obvious ramification of such a statement is the reiteration of conspiratorial models of masculinity, chiefly violent and combative. Coughlin can use more constructive words like "assertive" if he likes, but these gloss over the simple truth that contemporary Christian masculinity is largely a *military* masculinity. And just like the argument about "noble warriors" and "spiritual warriors" in the previous Archetypes chapter, there is no getting away from the fact that this is all about killing (whether spiritually/metaphorically or literally). Various forms of the Christian men's movement are effectively paramilitary organizations, framing their language, aesthetics and even props (everything from symbolic swords to target practice) in military terms. Further still, I have recently undertaken a study analyzing how Christian masculinity is also framed by animal hunting and meat consumption, which puts a very real bloody spin on otherwise metaphorical activities.

The appeal to "Biblical masculinity" is itself also problematic. As demonstrated in the previous Archetypes chapter with the story of King David, the Hebrew Bible is populated by all manner of nutters, rapists and murderers, dating right back to the story of Cain and Abel. God Himself in this text is often wrathful, patriarchal and unforgiving. Following the critical points of the History chapter, just because we have seen such precedents for thousands of years, it does not mean they are natural and inevitable (let alone divinely ordained).

When we get into the New Testament, Biblical masculinity gets more complicated. Yes, just as Coughlin argues, the kick-ass assertive Jesus does exist (we all get a thrill out of him driving the moneychangers out of the temple, for example). But both Jesus and other men in the Gospels are also often gentle and wracked with doubt. Indeed, contemporary scholarship of masculinity across all Christian sacred texts (and historical periods) demonstrates one big counter-conspiratorial claim: Biblical masculinity is wildly diverse, encompassing almost every point you can imagine (including eunuchs and men who may or may not even be human!). So ironically, the contemporary Christian claim about there being some kind of singular and authentic Biblical masculinity does nothing by expose a fundamental lack of understanding when it comes to reading the Bible. (Don't read this an anti-Christian statement, by the way. I'm largely pro-God: I just get annoyed by the kind of thinking that refuses to acknowledge the epic complexity of Christianity and most other faiths.)

Another interesting point is illuminated when we start to explore the nature of "masculine spirituality." Two academic studies about masculinity and spirituality unwittingly highlight the issue of what is and is not "masculine" (and even "spiritual") in these conversations. In an article, "Male spirituality and the men's movement: A factorial examination of motivations" in the journal *Psychology and Theology*, J. D. Castellini and colleagues identified the following motivations for men's involvement with spirituality which are here ordered in a way that arguably moves from the most spiritual to the least: relationship with God; faith/prayer community; self-awareness, or relationship with self; isolation or existential emptiness; fear or grief; father–son relationships; coping strategies; male bonding, or relationships with other men.

The results of the study showed, "the factor accounting for the largest portion of the shared variances was that of Male Bonding, or relationships with other men." Interestingly, of the motivations Castellini identified, only two (relationship with God and faith/prayer community) can accurately be described as spiritual. All the other motivations could equally be discussed in exclusively non-spiritual contexts. Of the motivations Castellini identified, only two (father–son relationships and male bonding) are uniquely "masculine" (in terms of pertaining only to men), and neither of these count among the two motivations that are uniquely spiritual. In Castellini's findings there is *no single variable* that is at once uniquely masculine *and* spiritual, yet it confidently describes "male spirituality."

Similar conclusions can be drawn from an article, "Ten Tenets of Male Spirituality" in *The Journal of Men's Studies* by Ian M. Harris, who undertook several surveys among predominantly Christian men. The ten tenets identified are: finding inner wisdom; searching for truth; speaking from the heart; confronting the dark side; loving; working for a better world; passing a test; belonging to something great; following scripture; believing in destiny. Harris locates these tenets within a spiritual context, but even Atheist Fundamentalists (Richard Dawkins, I'm talking to you) could happily sign up for all but the last two (following scripture and believing in destiny). As it is, the participants of Harris' study ranked those two tenets as the least important. The highest ranked tenet was "belonging to something great," which is not inherently spiritual. Furthermore, not one of those tenets is "masculine" or "male": they are simply factors that influenced the study participants who happen to be men. Rather than "Ten Tenets of Male Spirituality," Harris has actually defined "Ten Tenets of Spirituality Perceived By Some Men": a perfectly worthy exercise, but of a very different nature and one which again does not exactly describe a uniquely "male spirituality."

What both these studies demonstrate is that the conspiratorial claims about "masculine spirituality" do not stand up to even cursory examination. Let's put aside the issue of what does and does not count as spirituality, as this is another debate that rightly belongs in a different book called *The Spirituality Conspiracy*, and focus instead on masculinity. Six out of eight of

Castellini's motivations had nothing to do with even a normative understanding of masculinity (in other words, connected with being a man). Similarly, all ten of Harris' tenets could be experienced equally by men and women.

Let's then look at those aspects of masculinity tabled by Coughlin, such as assertiveness. *Why* is assertiveness masculine? Because the conspiracy says so? Because it is "natural" in men but not in women? Those are not compelling reasons to me. What we are seeing here is that the very meaning of what is and is not masculine is not just socially constructed, but also problematic in one of two ways: first, *the meaning assigned to masculinity is completely arbitrary*; second, *the meaning assigned to masculinity proactively serves the ends of the conspiracy* (the ultimate agenda of which we will unpack further in the next—concluding—chapter).

Fox's book provides some good examples of this seeming conundrum. Remember those ten metaphors of which Fox writes: Father Sky; the Green Man; Icarus and Daedalus; Hunter-Gatherers; Spiritual Warriors; Masculine Sexuality, Numinous Sexuality; Cosmic and Animal Bodies; the Blue Man; Earth Father; Grandfather Sky. Fox has done a better job of making his metaphors "masculine" by connecting them specifically with men's roles and images of men (albeit glossing over the sex/gender distinction we explored in the Introduction chapter). As such his "ten metaphors to awaken the sacred masculine" seem, initially, more intuitively correct than Coughlin's values which happen to have been assigned to men. But this is simply a cursory gesture that is not immune to the fundamental question of *why*?

Why are the values behind Father Sky, the Green Man and any other of Fox's metaphors masculine? Because they are values performed by men? This reasoning makes no sense. What happens, for example, when a man and a woman both embody the value of nurturing? Is nurturing a feminine value for the woman, and a masculine value for the man? If this is the case then there are no inherently masculine or feminine values, rather gender-free values that happen to be performed and embodied by men and women. Or is it the case that we are witnessing a man embodying a feminine value? If this is the case then please provide me with a compelling argument as to why nurturing is *inherently* feminine. I'm waiting... Remember, too, that we're talking here within the context of nurturing, but this reasoning extends to *each and every* theme and value we have examined in this book.

Now here's the tricky bit, but it's an important revealing as it highlights the sleight of hand or slippage on behalf of the conspiracy between the natural and the artificial. There *is* a point where values become gendered, but it's *not* the point being made by any of the texts I have analyzed here with you. Nurturing, for example, becomes gendered in a man or a woman's *experience* of nurturing. By this I mean that men and women live under the conspiracy that treats men and women—via constructions of masculine and feminine—differently.

A man and a woman may experience nurturing in a gendered way because the conspiracy has imposed on them a different relationship with nurturing. In other words, women's understanding and experience of nurturing is gendered by the conspiracy to be natural and inherent in their biological function of childbirth. Men's understanding and experience of nurturing is gendered by the conspiracy to be important but secondary to their social function of providing. *It is the experience and conspiratorial context of nurturing that is gendered, not the value of nurturing itself.* This is a really important distinction to keep in mind.

Another important distinction to keep in mind is that notion of balance and complementarity inherent in Fox's writing. This is the same note of caution made in the previous chapter about the Androgyne archetype, which while being an initially optimistic combination of "male strength and competence" and "female sensitivity and feeling" only ever consolidates the original conspiratorial categories of "male strength and competence" and "female sensitivity and feeling." Fox is a great example of many men I meet who genuinely want to get away from the kinds of conspiratorial masculinity this book is all about, but who remain trapped in conspiratorial binaries.

Thinking in relation to conspiratorial models of gender, even in order to mitigate then, usually results in the perpetuation of those binaries. As the feminist philosopher Judith Butler states in her book *Undoing Gender*, "to be not quite masculine or not quite feminine is still to be understood exclusively in terms of one's relationship to the 'quite masculine' and the 'quite feminine.'" *If you do not like the way masculinity is defined by the conspiracy, do not look to balance it with the way femininity is defined by the conspiracy: reject both.*

So to recap, there are various problems with the way spirituality is mobilized by the conspiracy:

- The assertion that Christianity is being "feminized" is really a symptom of anxiety about the loss of male power within this particular faith tradition.

- The Christian masculinity promoted by Coughlin is largely militaristic in nature, which in the end is distilled to violence.

- Far from being something singular and definitive, "Biblical masculinity" is a diverse spectrum of masculinities that ironically counter conspiratorial claims to "real" or "authentic" masculinity.

- The "values" behind masculine spirituality are often not masculine at all, and are assigned as such only to further the agenda of the conspiracy.

- The desire to seek balance and complementarity within a conspiratorial understanding of masculine and feminine does little but consolidate that conspiratorial understanding of masculine and feminine.

The Solution

There are two streams of thought that comprise the solution: one simple, the other less so. First, as we have seen above, a good deal of the conspiracy in the context of spirituality is exactly the same as we saw in the previous chapter in the context of archetypes. As such, the jumping off point of the solution involves not thinking archetypally. A small tweak to meaning—as we saw with Fox—is insufficient. It is not enough to offer a slightly less pathological archetype or change the word from archetype to metaphor and hope this will solve the problem. It requires radically shifting how we think about archetypes to mobilize the nuance suggested by the archetypal or elemental field, rather than the pathologically simplistic models of masculinity they otherwise suggest. Or you may just want to abandon all reference to archetypes or metaphors in relation to masculinity (my personal preference).

This rejection of archetypal thinking also extends to the Bible. Whether or not the stories of the Bible are real, we read them today mediated through a text that has been culturally and politically constructed over many hundreds of years. I really rather like the idea that Jesus was real and kicked ass in the temple with the moneychangers, but that account has to be seen for what it is: a Chinese whispers snapshot of Jesus' character in the moment, not a representation of his full self (human, divine, or otherwise). And of course, if you are going to read the Bible as inspiration, it is rather poor reasoning to cherry pick conspiratorially masculine images of Jesus being wild, when there are just as many moments of humility and feet-washing. Further still, the story of men in the Bible is so much bigger than Jesus: what a glorious spectrum of masculine characters it contains: betrayers, doubters, lovers and any number of other positions that make men the diverse, broken and visionary things that they are. In short, the solution lies in reading the Bible with greater depth and sophistication.

The second part of the solution deals with addressing the anxiety that spirituality is a largely feminine phenomenon. On an intuitive level this concern is quite reasonable (but remember what I said in the Introduction chapter about intuitive responses often being little more than conditioning responses). Yes, it is true that there are fewer men than women sat in the pews of the average congregation. Yes, it is true that outside organized religion, spirituality appears to be "feminine." For example, I recently gave a talk at the MindBodySpirit Festival in Melbourne, and noticed there were a number of stalls which referred to products about Goddesses and the feminine, but not one that referred to Gods or the masculine. And nearly all the stalls were built around a pastel or crystal-type aesthetic which resonates with a stereotypically feminine spirituality.

The intuitive response to this anxiety has been to counter those stereotypically "feminine" spiritual phenomena with the equally stereotypical "masculine." Spiritual writers and men in leadership positions know that men have just as much need and ability to be spiritual as women, and in order to enable this they frame the spiritual as "masculine," assuming this is what men desire. This is why we see Christian men's ministries built around a wild Jesus, paramilitary themes and sport. This is why we see alternative spiritualities built around spiritual warriors and the erect phallus of the Green Man.

Let's assume for a moment that this concern is valid (rather than there being innumerable men who, due to social conditioning, simply articulate and embody their spirituality in less obvious ways). The primary challenge is how do we bring more men to the table? The overriding answer, as we have seen, has been to make the spiritual more "manly." But the danger with this is that it has a habit of consolidating all those conspiratorial models of masculinity. But there is another way of looking at this: instead of assuming spirituality is the changeable variable that can be shifted into line with men, why not consider that men are the changeable variable that can be shifted into line with spirituality? After all, we have already seen that masculinity is socially constructed: it is malleable like putty.

But, comes the outcry, this results in denying masculine values and turning men into pastel-colored crystal-wearing lady men! Even worse than Mansfield's gender-neutral society, this results in an unambiguous feminine society! Not so, of course. Or rather, yes it *is* about denying masculine values, but only inasmuch as those values are *described* as masculine, rather than denying those values in themselves. This is a reiteration of the point made previously about nurturing, but I'm going to say it again slightly differently, because it is of fundamental importance to both thinking critically about the problem, and proactively constructing the solution.

Let's assume, for the sake of argument, that spirituality is defined by two values (clearly there are many more): immanence (which is generally perceived to be feminine) and transcendence (which is generally perceived to be masculine). In the current formula, immanence is considered to be the more popular value, it is considered feminine by society and therefore spirituality is more appealing to women. In the current formula, to win more men to spirituality, transcendence is beefed up to almost comical proportions and thus, goes the theory, we reach some kind of holism in which both men and women are having their spiritual needs met.

But what if immanence was not perceived as feminine and transcendence was not perceived as masculine? I am not talking here about doing away with either of these values, simply unhooking them from a gendered expectation. If immanence was considered equally masculine as feminine in orientation, and also a popular value within contemporary ways of "doing" spirituality, would we not experience those people of masculine orientation (largely—although not exclusively—men) being more involved in spirituality? I think we would. Certainly, if you are aiming to attract greater numbers of men to spirituality it is a more daunting task to change the way people think in general about gender than it is to make a few spiritual spaces more "manly," but ultimately it is more useful.

In short, this results in there being no such thing as "masculine spirituality." Importantly, however, this does not mean that what are perceived as masculine values are erased, simply that they are no longer described as masculine. But there is a further challenge here, especially for progressive-minded men and women. I suspect that I can sell you the idea of there being no such thing as masculine spirituality with relative ease because of the way I have presented it here: in other words, no one is that fussed if we do away with wildness, paramilitary themes and sport, as they're often considered a bit weird anyway.

However, the other side of the coin is that there is also no such thing as "feminine spirituality." Again, this does not mean that what are perceived as feminine values are erased, simply that they are no longer described as feminine. How does that sound, particularly to a second-wave feminist worldview? No more women's spirituality, no more feminine nurturing, weaving, immanence, healing, and so on. Of course, this does not stop conversations about women's *experience* of spirituality. Feminist spirituality, for example, still exists, but this would be about how women's experience of the spiritual is regulated and liberated within a patriarchal culture, rather than some kind of spirituality that is inherent in women due to their biological sex. (There are some feminist spiritualities that already assume this to be the case, while others hang on to women's biological specificity. Despite the claims of writers such as Mansfield who resist "feminism" as if it were one thing, feminisms—in the plural—are extremely diverse and sometimes even contradictory).

A similar process takes place when we look at "gay spirituality" in the context of masculinity. Have a look at this creedal statement about gay men that underpins gay spirituality as defined by Harry Hay (who is commonly understood as the founder of the gay men's movement):

- They are *not*, by nature, territorially aggressive and do not impose their political claims on others.

- They are *not*, by nature, competitive but are passionately interested in sharing with others.

- They are *not* interested in conquering nature but are interested in harmonious living with all of nature.

- They are *not* interested in denying bodiliness and carnality but are passionately involved in celebrating all aspects of human sexuality.

Just as the "gay" Androgyne archetype in the previous chapter described by Toby Johnson did not involve any aspect bound with same-sex desire, so too Hay's description. We see here a range of "gay" values that can easily be unhooked from gayness and applied to all people, a process which offers a powerful counter-conspiratorial solution. What such a process does is keep these values—along with nurturing, weaving, immanence, healing, transcendence and spiritual warriors—on the table, but open to people of both masculine and feminine orientation, open to both men and women, open to both gay and straight.

This process is a win–win. On the one hand, it provides a mechanism to enable more men back into the spiritual domain, easing the anxiety of those who believe there are not enough men in the church. (However, keep in mind that if those anxious men have a problem with this suggestion, their concern is exposed as not being about the *number* of men in the church, rather the *absence of power* that a conspiratorial masculinity wields within the church.) And on the other hand, it rejects the claim of the conspiracy that masculinity is defined in a particular way, enabling men (and, indeed, women of a masculine orientation) to choose whichever values happen to fit their character and spiritual worldview.

Spirituality (and I use the term as a shorthand to include both orthodox organized religions and the spectrum of unorthodox alternatives) is at once a prime site of regulation *by* the conspiracy and liberation *from* the conspiracy. For thousands of years spiritualities have perpetuated the conspiracy, whether it be their explicit patriarchal nature that excludes women from positions of influence and power, their encouragement of a militaristic and oppressive masculinity, or their rendering of "new age" products as stereotypically feminine. Yet what else is more appropriate when we are seeking solutions to liberate ourselves from conspiratorial constructions of masculine and feminine than a domain that is simultaneously inherent in but also points beyond constructions of self-identity?

Spirituality, at the very least, provides an extraordinary *thinking space* for how the self might look. Most people know, for example, that when they refer to God in a traditional bearded-man-on-a-throne way, that image is not literal, rather something *that stands in* for God, a concept that is far more complex and which may even extend beyond the limits of language and human understanding into the ineffable (that which cannot be articulated). Spirituality, then, is a domain in which we are already used to taking what we know, recognizing its limitations, and then striving to think beyond them.

We can employ this same process with gender. Yes, we have a strong imagine of masculinity as defined by the conspiracy, yet we know this is not literal (remember the "don't identify too much with the archetype" problem), rather something *that stands in* for masculinity, a concept that is far more complex and which may even extend beyond the limits of language and human understanding. I don't say this just for literary effect. I genuinely find the more time I spend with this subject, the more I hit a wall of language and meaning about what *gender is all about*. Yes, I can identify clearly enough how it is constructed, regulated and even how it should be liberated. But it is a far more elusive task to identify what is *real*, and what is just some made up consensus, like the value of tulip bulbs in seventeenth century Holland.

Spirituality, then, provides us with a useful way of thinking about the self at the edge of meaning, peering into what may be real or what may be fantasy, but with the knowledge that the eventual answer to this conundrum is less important than the journey, the process of questioning, and the continually unfolding revelations that result. That's a pretty good model to follow as we leave behind the masculinity conspiracy and begin to both individually and collectively discover who we really are.

8: CONCLUSION

The Conspiracy

In the very first paragraph of this book I asked you to look in a mirror. I asked you to contemplate certain details and to notice that there is an increasingly large disconnect between who you feel you are and the person in the mirror, a distance between the two yous that is difficult to articulate in words. I then asked you to imagine that gap between the mirror and every man in the world alive right now, then for every man who has ever lived. That's a lot of disconnect, a vast space between men and the men in the mirror.

This is largely a thinking exercise about perception and how easy it is to realize that what you think you know—your image in the mirror—can swiftly be called into question. If we can acknowledge that new perceptions can be established even in our own reflection, then we can acknowledge that new perceptions can be established in *all* aspects of our identify. But there's also a more literal sense to this disconnect between men and the men in the mirror. The masculinity conspiracy is chiefly a dissociative exercise: it forces an unwanted space between men and their potential in order to pursue its own ends (which we will explore shortly). Let's briefly look back on the previous chapters to see where these spaces are constructed:

- Within the context of history the dissociative space is constructed by tethering men to the past. The conspiracy argues there are innumerable historical precedents for its model of masculinity, demonstrating it is not just culturally and socially determined, but also biologically determined.

- Within the context of sexuality the dissociative space is constructed by tethering men to sexual polarity. The conspiracy argues that men's rightful sexuality is defined chiefly by assertiveness in opposition to women's sexual receptivity.

- Within the context of relationships the dissociative space is constructed by tethering men to specific relational dynamics. The conspiracy argues that men and women think and communicate differently and that these differences must be decoded and mastered in order for men to be successful with women.

- Within the context of fatherhood the dissociative space is constructed by tethering men to a narrow understanding of boyhood. The conspiracy argues that boys develop in particular ways and that to ignore this is to rob them of their true nature.

- Within the context of archetypes the dissociative space is constructed by tethering men to simplistic behavioral templates. The conspiracy argues there are a small number of mythical or metaphorical models of manhood to emulate that encapsulate its true essence.

- Within the context of spirituality the dissociative space is constructed by tethering men to Biblical masculinity. The conspiracy argues that sacred texts provide a divinely ordained model of masculinity that does not only show men how to behave, but resists the feminization of faith and society in general.

In each chapter I have unraveled some of the initial problems with these lines of thought, and provided some solutions for re-thinking them in more useful ways, all the while opening up a more fruitful space for *your own* visions of counter-conspiratorial masculinity rather than a specific alternative.

However, the conspiracy has done a very good job of convincing both men and women that its vision of masculinity is correct. It has, after all, operated in most places throughout most times. But it does not rest on its laurels. It continually regulates the domain over which it reigns and asserts in a mantra-like fashion phrases like "real," "authentic," or "true" masculinity. It also continually seeks out other domains in which to function, and is very clever at describing all sorts of "new," "evolved," and "counter-cultural" masculinities that continue to perpetuate conspiratorial values, turning over old orthodoxies and creating new ones. The conspiracy is dead! Long live the conspiracy!

Throughout this book I have shown you numerous examples of the conspiracy *at work*. But let's dig a bit deeper into *how* the conspiracy works. Remember Michael Barkun's description of conspiracy thinking from the introductory chapter? Barkun states it is characterized by three chief elements. First, *nothing happens by accident*: there is always intent behind actions; the willed nature of reality is paramount. Second, *nothing is as it seems*: the source of a conspiracy tends to conceal its activities through the appearance of innocence or misinformation. Third, *everything is connected*: patterns abound in conspiracy; exposing conspiracy is about unveiling these hidden connections.

I confess that when I initially mobilized the conspiracy motif it was done so rather cynically. While I was genuinely interested in finding a different way of discussing masculinity that moved beyond the binary proposed on the one hand by feminists and on the other hand by men's rights advocates, I was also simply hoping to capture the imagination of readers who were into conspiracy books. Conspiracy logic as defined by Barkun seemed reasonably applicable to gender politics, so I used it. But as I have finished each chapter of this book, I have fallen more into line with the idea that the conspiracy motif *is far more applicable* than I originally imagined.

As we have seen throughout the text, *nothing happens by accident*. Each chapter has demonstrated that while the conspiracy claims its presentation of masculinity is simply the way things are, a specific and proactive agenda is being fulfilled. As we have seen throughout the text, *nothing is as it seems*: Each chapter has demonstrated that while the conspiracy claims its presentation of masculinity is natural and inevitable, there are clear alternatives, and not just imagined and theoretical alternatives, but ones that are surprisingly easy to embody. And as we have seen throughout the text, *everything is connected*: Each chapter has demonstrated that while the conspiracy claims to be based on "evidence" and "science," this is often a closed ecology of connected people and ideas that simply choose not to consider conflicting options, referring instead only to those who confirm their worldview.

But how does the conspiracy pull it off? How has it managed to perpetuate itself so successfully for so many centuries and in so many places? Answering that question is in itself another book. Today, one of the chief problems with the conspiracy is that it robs us of the ability to even realize it is in operation. This is what all the "real," "authentic," and "true" language is all about. The conspiracy is framed not as a specific regulatory dynamic with a particular agenda; rather, there is no conspiracy, only *the way that it is*. By concealing the fact that it even exists—by appealing to the supposedly "natural" and "common sense"—the conspiracy hides in plain sight. There are some nice fictional precedents for this tactic. Think, for example, of the movie *The Usual Suspects* in which the villain, Keyser Söze, secures the potency of his evil persona by creating an aura of doubt about his existence. As he sits before his clueless interrogator, Söze transparently shares his methodology with the memorable line, "the greatest trick the devil ever pulled was convincing the world he didn't exist." (The more literary among you may prefer the same point as made earlier by C. S. Lewis, and before him Charles Baudelaire).

Further still, the conspiracy robs us of the critical thinking skills required to identify that it is hiding in plain sight in the first place, let alone to do something about it. This is achieved by the extraordinary dumbing down of information around us, which I have referred to in earlier chapters. It has been an interesting exercise as this book has been published online to witness a small but persistent number of readers complain that the style of writing is too complex and "intellectual." On various occasions I have been asked to cut out the jargon, make it easier to read, provide allegedly "real life examples" and so on, which would all bring the text more into line with the kind of self-help books many folks seem to have become conditioned to expect.

The impression seems to be that this is an "academic" book trying to pass itself off a something altogether different. But this is genuinely not the case. If you think this writing is academic, you clearly have not read much academic writing lately (which often I can't figure out either). The demand for ever-simpler writing, bullet points, instant insights, micro-summaries and so forth render books incapable of addressing the complexity of the issues at hand. Masculinity is a complex issue: you might think some of the popular writers are writing about it with "clarity," but they are simply stripping it of all subtlety and nuance. It's certainly desirable to aim for clarity, but at some point compromise becomes fatal: it might result in a slot on Oprah's couch, but it will not result in anything useful. Complex issues require appropriately complex handling.

More than this, the status quo critiqued here *requires* people not to think with appropriate complexity, subtlety and nuance in order to perpetuate its nonsense agenda. So when I hear complaints about the book being too complex, my immediate thought is not that I've failed in my task to clearly communicate, rather that the reader is showing how far they are conditioned into the conspiracy (a classic example of conspiratorial logic, if ever there was one!). It also seems a bit fishy to me when critics will focus on what they claim to be stylistic problems rather than the topics under discussion, which seems a rather transparent diversion tactic.

Instead of meeting the reader behind such complaints fully on their ground, I ask them to meet me half way (as I have already moved from my natural domain into the middle ground). In doing so we collectively claw back some of the critical thinking territory lost in our dumbed-down world. My aim, too, in writing in an appropriately complex manner is to pay readers the respect they deserve in assuming they are capable of understanding complex issues: an important but increasingly rare gesture. I find that in my face-to-face communications with people (often in rather random circumstances) I can get into some really quite complex territory, the like of which it is assumed they are not capable of reading in books. This assumption was made even clearer to me recently on receiving comments from several "professional" readers from an unnamed mind-body-spirit publisher who read *The Masculinity Conspiracy*. Have a look at the following feedback:

- Reader 1: *I like the style*. My question is how much more is it than an extended book(s) review, (most of which I haven't read, so confess ignorance in the area), and *how we're going to sell it*.

- Reader 2: Love the short blurb, it immediately made me want to read the book. *Extremely well written* in a reader friendly way that makes even someone completely uninterested in the subject sit up and take notice. The book certainly makes some good points and although it examines other books on the subject it does so in a style which, although serious, is light and sometimes humorous. I found this an enjoyable read and it made me stop and think and in doing so I realized that a part of my mind had already explored these issues but without having anywhere to express them. I'm not sure *how many people would actually buy it*.

- Reader 3: I agree, *well written, great style and an interesting subject*, but general *sales will be a problem*.

This is an excellent example of how the conspiracy regulates society. Here we have three professional readers who all seem to like the book, but they can't imagine anyone else liking it! Certainly, they know the market and what people tend to buy. But people buy largely in accordance with their conditioning by the conspiracy, so to narrowly serve that market is to serve the conspiracy. This is forgivable for people who do not know any better, but I find it troubling that people who knowingly like a counter-conspiratorial text choose not to publish it, as this is nothing short of spineless collaboration. One could be forgiven for thinking it was not that these readers *could not imagine* anyone else liking the book, rather *they did not want* anyone else liking the book. But that would be the kind of paranoia Barkun identifies as being symptomatic of conspiratorial thinking, rather than exposing it :) Instead, endless books are published and celebrated that both perpetuate conspiratorial values and congratulate readers for being in agreement, which in turn makes readers feel better about those values, and thus that closed ecology of ideas continues.

This leads to the final twist in the act of self-concealment: despite all the dumbing down, the conspiracy will often paradoxically give the impression that the people it dupes are extremely clever. Barkun echoes this point in his description of conspiracy thinking, noting that it will often mimic mainstream scholarship (I spoke a bit about the use of the term "research" and flaky PhDs back in the Relationships chapter). Not only do conspiracy writers give the impression they are extremely clever, citing other fancy writers, describing themselves as "philosophers" and perhaps belonging to some kind of vaporous Institute of Evolved Personhood (often little more than a paper entity with a bank account set up to accept donations and workshop fees), they also talk about their *followers* as being extremely clever. This is a cunning maneuver as it at once makes people feel very special for agreeing with the conspiratorial worldview, implies that if you do not agree with it you must *not* be very clever, and neutralizes momentum to move beyond it to something genuinely clever (or, more accurately, and as we shall see next, something elegantly simple, because while the machinations of the conspiracy are complex, its ultimate source is not).

In sum, the conspiracy functions via numerous sleights of hand:

- Through its prescriptive vision of masculinity the conspiracy produces a forced space between men and their potential.

- By giving the impression that there is no conspiracy— *simple the way things are*—the conspiracy hides in plain sight.

- By robbing us of the critical thinking skills required to identify it exists, the conspiracy prevents us from imagining a viable alternative.

The Problem

But identifying how the conspiracy manifests—and even how it functions—is not the end of the story. Indeed, the chief problem remains: *what is ultimately behind the conspiracy?* When talking about this with people there is often an assumption that I am doing something very simply here: namely, using the word "conspiracy" instead of "patriarchy." That initially sounds quite plausible, as a good number of the points I have made in this book are based on a feminist analysis of patriarchy. Others points are based on an understanding of "hegemonic masculinity" as described by Raewyn Connell, which is about how men regulate themselves as well as women in relation to time-honored ways of being a man. Still others are based on queer theory, which is about subverting and demonstrating the fluidity of meaning that surrounds terms like "masculinity." All these ways of looking at gender foreground patriarchy, so it is certainly a reasonable assumption that patriarchy *is* the conspiracy. But it is only a partial answer.

While understanding patriarchy is a crucial aspect of exposing the conspiracy, we have to move past typically entrenched positions on this subject. In debates surrounding men and masculinities, there are two commonly held positions on patriarchy. On the one hand are those with feminist sympathies who talk about patriarchy, and how this marginalizes and oppresses women (and atypical men). On the other hand are men's rights advocates who identify the many problems suffered by men in society (such as poor health and education standards, violence, incarceration, social isolation, suicide, and so on) and simply do not see claims about patriarchy as valid any more.

But there is a way to reconcile these two seemingly opposed positions. Yes, it is true that patriarchy exists, but patriarchy is not the conspiracy, rather *patriarchy is mobilized by the conspiracy*. The conspiracy co-opts men to oppress women, a statement which supports the feminist claim that patriarchy operates as a regulating force within society. But, paradoxically, the conspiracy has little interest in men as individuals, which explains why men simultaneously enjoy the benefits of systemic privilege while often being on the shitty end of the stick as individuals. (There is *a lot* more complexity to be unpacked in this paragraph, but this will have to wait for another time).

It is crucial for those with a feminist worldview to realize that patriarchy is ultimately a tool of the conspiracy, not an end in itself. And while there are only few radical separatist feminists around these days, it is therefore important to acknowledge that there is *nothing inherently bad about men*, simply that they have been co-opted by the conspiracy in such an extraordinarily effective way that they usually don't even realize it has happened. Of course, this does not absolve men of the ills wrought by patriarchy, nor of the requirement to counter its oppressive effects. It is also crucial for those with a men's rights worldview to acknowledge that patriarchy does exist, to understand the complexity that comes with owning systemic privilege (the kind of thing that still results in men often earning more money than women for the same job) and understanding this is different to individual privilege (from which individual men may or may benefit).

Clearly, if patriarchy is not the conspiracy then there must be some higher—overarching—force (maybe even, according to Barkun's original conspiratorial formula, a "demonic force"). There are plenty of people I speak to who, having agreed that patriarchy is not the conspiracy, then swiftly move on to the conclusion that it is *capitalism* that is the conspiracy. There is, after all, a long-standing Marxist tradition that shows how capitalism is the driving oppressive force in society, and it is easy to imagine that it is *this* that mobilizes patriarchy in the way described above. There are other contenders too: classism, racism, and so on. All these contenders either mobilize patriarchy in some way, or we can imagine how the conspiracy is using them as a vehicle for perpetuating its prescriptive vision for masculinity.

All these contenders are reasonable, but the conspiracy ultimately works on a broader level still. And it's nothing obscure or esoteric, nothing that requires a PhD in developmental psychology or political science to understand. The conspiracy is simply *power and domination*. A good place to get a description of this is Walter Wink's *Engaging the Powers: Discernment and Resistance in a World of Domination* (a quick nod to Luke Devlin, whose comments on earlier online chapters drew the Wink connection). Wink is a theologian, so genuinely tends towards the forces at hand being "demonic" and our salvation from them being of the literal variety. However, the way he *describes* power and domination is also largely valid from an atheistic point of view.

Wink argues there has been a domination myth at the heart of humanity that dates back thousands of years in which "might makes right." Quite early in his book, Wink also tables a version of the masculinity conspiracy, stating "this myth also inadvertently reveals the price men have paid for power they acquired over women: complete servitude to their earthly rules and gods. Women for their part were identified with inertia, chaos, and anarchy."

So the conspiracy is an abstract assertion of power and domination over people at an individual, institutional and systemic level (in other words, at *every* level). In our present context, the conspiracy demands a particular form of masculinity that lends itself towards domination (think again of all the references we've heard about aggression, assertiveness, warriors, and so on) and mobilizes men to put that domination to work against women and other men via various methods such as patriarchy.

But in exactly the same way that the conspiracy constructs a particular form of masculinity (demonstrating its changeability), so too is the conspiracy itself constructed. Wink argues the domination myth took hold through various accidents of social and cultural construction and warfare (and, importantly for Wink, humanity's Fall from grace in the eyes of God), to the point where it seemed ingrained in human nature. This does not mean that domination is inherent in humanity, simply that it was forced up on it, as noted by Wink: "The struggle for domination meant that many humane cultural options that people might have preferred were closed off. The self-interests of individuals were subordinated, often even sacrificed, to the interests of the larger systems in which they were embedded."

Identifying how the conspiratorial machine operates then becomes increasingly simple. Domination as the myth of default human behavior took hold, and we can see how this filters across society. Wink claims, "power lost by men through submission to a ruling elite was compensated by power gained over women, children, hired workers, slaves, and the land." In that sentence alone we see our previous contenders for the conspiracy: patriarchy, capitalism, class, race, and how they all serve the domination myth.

The domination myth became the consensus reality, taking on a life of its own: this is why it is impossible to identify a "person" behind the conspiracy, because the conspiracy is the sum of all our actions and complicity within the domination myth. Further still, Wink argues that even the leaders who run the various modes of domination do not have genuine agency in the matter: their roles are conferred upon them by the domination system. For Wink, "people have thus become slaves of their own evolving systems, rather than civilized society being the servant of its members."

In order for such a false consensus reality to take hold, we—as actors in this conspiratorial drama—must allow ourselves to be blinkered by the conspiracy. Or, in the parlance again of *The Matrix* movie, we must choose to take the blue pill: "wake up in your bed and believe whatever you want to believe." Wink claims that "whatever the System tells our brains is real is what we are allowed to notice; everything else must be ignored." This explains how the "natural" and "common sense" appear to prevail in the conspiracy, despite there being easy-to-grasp alternatives: our conspiracy-conditioned brains simply cannot see them, they must be ignored.

Have you ever been faced by a large quandary (let's say third world poverty) that seems so blindingly easy to fix (a more equitable distribution of global capital), but the solution seems so obvious and simple that you feel it must be wrong—otherwise we'd be doing it, right? That's the domination myth at work: the consensus reality it constructs will not allow us to accept the blindingly obvious solution. Similarly, the conspiracy will not allow us to accept the blindingly obvious alternatives to the model of masculinity it demands.

For many, the real horror is not that this has happened throughout human history (although this is bad enough), but rather coming to the realization that this trick has been pulled on us personally and our role within it. Wink states, "It is only after we experience liberation from primary socialization to the world-system that we realize how terribly we have violated our authentic personhood—and how violated we have been." For some, the horror is too great: Plug me back into the matrix! For others, the pulling back of the curtain to see the "great" wizard is a genuinely empowering revelation: I have met people who have woken up to this fact and rapidly changed their lives in fundamental ways.

So to recap, while it is important to understand how the conspiracy *works* in terms of masculinity, it is also important to understand *what is actually behind the conspiracy*:

- The conspiracy mobilizes patriarchy by encouraging men to oppress women (and atypical men), but paradoxically has little interest in men as individuals.

- Patriarchy is not the conspiracy, nor are other plausible-sounding contenders such as capitalism, classism and racism.

- *Power and domination* are at the heart of the conspiracy.

- The domination myth is simply a consensus realty. Despite the claims of the conspiracy, *it is not natural or inevitable*.

The Solution

Our challenge, of course, is what we then do about it, this thing that has had us duped for most—if not all—of human history.

The good news for us is that we do not necessarily have to immediately construct glorious alternatives to bring about great change, rather simply withdraw our support from the conspiratorial status quo. Wink cites the sixteenth-century French political philosopher Étienne de La Boétie who wrote in reference to the masses who allowed themselves to be hoodwinked by rulers who really had very little power over them: "I do not ask that you place hand upon the tyrant to topple him over, but simply that you support him no longer; then you will behold him, like a great colossus whose pedestal has been pulled away, fall of his own weight and break into pieces."

I'm not sure it's *quite* that simple, but it's an excellent start. In order to withdraw our support we need to firstly and primarily start *thinking differently*. This is the point where I often hear people moan about over-intellectualizing at the expense of action. But this too is the conspiracy speaking through the person in front of me, a cunning act of ventriloquism. If we do not firstly create a new thinking space *there can be no useful action*. Without the thinking space we are either rendered impotent by the conspiracy and do nothing, or we act without sufficient thought, both of which play expertly into the hands of the conspiracy.

Creating new thinking spaces allows us two equally valuable options. First is the obvious path of significantly changing our lifestyles. More people than you imagine do this. I have met a number of people who live radically counter-cultural lifestyles who were once some kind of deeply entrenched cog in the machine. These folks are not, as is so easy to imagine, people who never bought into the system in the first place, folks chasing an endless adolescence and delaying the inevitable perils of settling down under the yoke of responsibility. These folks have woken up to the reality that *alternatives are possible* and take only a relatively minor leap of faith to manifest (relatively minor, that is, to the alternative of spending the rest of one's life being plugged into the matrix). I don't want to speak further here about specific alternatives because they depend on individual needs and desires, and I am more interested in catalyzing the thought processes for people to construct those alternatives for themselves.

Second, creating new thinking spaces allows us to think afresh about our current circumstances. You may, for example, perceive yourself to be an administrative drone working for some nameless organization. You don't need to pack it all in and move to a commune to embody a solution. The solution lies chiefly *in our interior*, and despite efforts to the contrary in various conspiratorial domains, this still belongs to us as free agents. And don't make the mistake of thinking that you're not a free agent, because you most certainly are. You may well be locked into a job and a mortgage with all manner or ties (some you're happy about, others you're not), *but you remain free to think yourself out of the conspiracy* while remaining in your current circumstances.

The conspiracy is a confidence trick, and it is surprisingly easy to call its bluff. Indeed, it may be more valuable to be an "enemy within" the system by reimagining your current circumstances than to opt out of them. You can create a quiet revolution: subtle re-thinking, transgression and subversion. You might be surprised at the liminal space you can make around you which, when connected with that of others, gently transforms rather than overturns the environments in which you live and work.

To create new thinking spaces we can return initially to the mirror. When we look in the mirror and begin to notice the disconnect between our interior and the person in the mirror, an obvious question bubbles to the surface of our consciousness: *Who am I?* Whether your worldview is spiritual or humanistic, this points to a fundamentally existential line of thought which is crucial to exposing the conspiracy. The conspiracy wants to tell you who you are, populating our interior with all those assumptions about masculinity (and femininity) we have worked through in the previous chapters. But the existential line of questioning has no time for such packaged answers: it wants to know the fundamental question: *Why?*

If you can, go and pick up a copy of Irvin Yalom's *Existential Psychotherapy* (actually, any of his books will probably do the job, and also be lighter to carry home from the library). Yalom does an excellent job of unpacking the four existential ultimate concerns: death, meaninglessness, isolation and freedom. (As it happens, I'm not convinced these four concerns are equally ultimate. For example, isolation and freedom are like water off a duck's back to me, but death and meaninglessness—two sides of the same coin—routinely keep me awake at night).

I would suggest if you have not wrangled with these issues at some point, you are not paying sufficient attention. Yalom demonstrates how many of our neuroses come down to trying to address these issues, often in unconscious or inarticulate ways. We grapple with death: how do we live in the face of death, what strategies do we employ in an attempt to cheat death? We grapple with meaning: How do we construct meaning, *what's the damn point of it all* if we're going to die anyway? We grapple with isolation: How do we navigate this bleak territory that keeps us isolated both from ourselves and other people? We grapple with freedom: How do we accept the horror that we are free to choose (and, indeed, have already chosen) or at least interpret the circumstances in which we find ourselves, rather than putting the blame elsewhere?

These four concerns alone are sufficient to fill a lifetime of contemplation and anxiety. I am told it is possible to move beyond this line of questioning and if not to find actual answers then at least make peace with the questions. I'm not convinced of this personally, but at 37 years old am nevertheless open to changing my mind on the matter at some period in the future when I have discovered mental tranquility :) The point is, this line of questioning will open up the thinking space necessary to counter the conspiracy. I don't care what your conclusions are at the moment: I'm simply suggesting they will at the very least disrupt the hold the conspiracy has over you. (Of course, it's not necessarily good: there are some dangerous conclusions, such as extremists who go to murderous lengths to demonstrate some kind of post-ethical freedom to be who they want to be). In short, existentialism is back!

Once we are routinely creating new thinking spaces we can begin to look outside of ourselves. Again, I'm not interested here in identifying specific solutions, rather making basic points that will enable those solutions to emerge within the experiences of you, the reader. On a number of occasions throughout this book I have stated that in the same way that there is a masculinity conspiracy, there is also a femininity conspiracy: As the flip-side of the conspiratorial coin, the masculinity conspiracy requires an equally prescriptive model of femininity to perpetuate its power grab. However, I firmly believe it is the masculinity conspiracy that is more problematic. While the femininity conspiracy asserts power in various ways (an example commonly perceived being the use of sex as a bargaining tool with men, and a shaming tool with other women), it does not have the power footprint of the masculinity conspiracy, which has mobilized patriarchy within our social and cultural systems, and which in turn has extended into a whopping ecological footprint on our planet.

As such, when looking outwards for solutions, *the primary agents in overturning the conspiracy must be men*. I'll say it again: the solution lies mostly with men. Of course, *this does not absolve women of responsibility*, it simply suggests men need to do *more* work than women. This requires two distinct steps. First, men need to own their individual privilege within patriarchy, and also their part in the systemic privilege that patriarchy confers upon them. Again, this may seem counter-intuitive to some men whose experience echoes the shocking statistics of men and poor health, violence, isolation and so on. But them's the breaks, and the conspiracy wants you to resist it as to do so continues its concealment. Second, once men have owned their role in patriarchy, they must do something about it: but, crucially, *not be shamed by it*.

There are a small number of men who, having discovered their complicity in patriarchy, become overwhelmingly shamed, and retreat into self-loathing. (This is the type of "mangina" perceived and bemoaned by hostile men's rights advocates. As it happens, most of those labeled as such are not bound by shame and self-loathing, rather men healthily seeking to counter patriarchy, but nevertheless it can be an issue.) This type of shamed individual sometimes has a habit of assuming women (and queer people) have the moral high-ground when it comes to issues about gender. As such, the solutions tend to have a focus towards *their* agency, when as much attention needs to be given to "regular" men's agency.

I have already mentioned this above in regard to the two commonly held positions in the gender debate, but I firmly believe the solution lies in getting men to understand that patriarchy paradoxically has little interest in them as individuals. There is a tremendous amount of energy within men's rights communities, but it is too often hostile towards women and feminism. Many of the problems those communities rightly identify are often blamed on the too-far-swung pendulum of women's gains in recent decades. But this is not the case. Women's gains *do not* come at the expense of men's; it is not a zero sum game. Women's gains have been earned by claiming what is rightfully and justly theirs: they have extracted this *from the conspiracy*, not from men.

I believe that once it becomes clear to men that they have been co-opted by the conspiracy into patriarchy to further the domination myth, and that it is *this* and not women's gains that is responsible for the problems men face in society, they will see the benefit of overturning both patriarchy and the conspiracy. And they will do so swiftly. All the energy that is currently wasted on finger-pointing from men's rights advocates can then be usefully spent elsewhere. I also believe that such a realization will allow the kind of healing in men's psyches that has been sought since the men's movement flourished in the early 1990s, but which to date has been misdirected by the conspiracy into concerns about the feminization of society.

However, while it is primarily men who must step up and counter the conspiracy, a further necessity is the realization that we are all in this together: men, women, gay, straight, and anyone who quite rightly resists such categorization. As gender and identity politics evolved over the past forty or so years it has been necessary for a certain amount of separatism to eventuate. Women and queer people, for example, needed to get together on their own, celebrate and assert their identities, and hold their oppressors accountable for the injustices dealt to them.

While it remains as important as ever for such specific voices to be heard, it is now necessary to complement these with strong alliances. This means moving beyond the women's movement, and beyond the men's movement, towards a people's movement. Do not hear me say that individual oppressed voices—such as women and queer people—should be in any way erased in such a movement. A people's movement is built precisely on the different experiences of its members: it celebrates and advocates for those differences. However, a people's movement is not defined by *specific differences*. A people's movement is defined by the assumption of *everybody's differences*. It is in such an alliance that the critical mass is achieved for a multiplicity of new thinking spaces and resulting actions that will overturn the conspiracy not just at the individual, but at the systemic level: the great colossus whose pedestal has been pulled away falls of his own weight and breaks into pieces.

And while the people's movement is born out of gendered identity, it does not stop there. It is inevitable that the kind of thought processes—and then actions—that go into supporting genuine gender difference extend into other domains, those other sites of oppression referred to above: class, race and so on. The people's movement demands freedom from power and domination wherever it operates. The people's movement shouts, "The emperor is wearing no clothes!" The people's movement calls the conspiracy's bluff. It's so simple, so elegant. And it all starts with looking in the mirror, and questioning who it is who looks back.

147

BIBLIOGRAPHY

Barkun, Michael. (2006). *A culture of conspiracy: Apocalyptic visions in contemporary America.* Berkeley, CA: University of California Press.

Bly, Robert. (1990). *Iron John: A book about men.* Reading, MA: Addison-Wesley.

Butler, Judith. (1999). *Gender trouble: Feminism and the subversion of identity* (2nd ed.). London: Routledge.

Butler, Judith. (2004). *Undoing gender.* London: Routledge.

Castellini, J. D., Nelson, W. M., Barrett, J. J., Nagy, M. S., & Quatman, G. L. (2005). Male spirituality and the men's movement: A factorial examination of motivations. *Psychology and Theology,* 33(1), 41-55.

Chatwin, Bruce. (1988). *The songlines.* New York: Penguin Books.

Connell, Raewyn., & Messerschmidt, J. W. (2005). Hegemonic masculinity: Rethinking the concept. *Gender & Society,* 19(6), 829-859.

Coughlin, Paul. (2005). *No more Christian nice guy: When being nice—instead of good—hurts men, women and children.* Minneapolis: Bethany House Publishers.

Culbertson, Phillip. (1993). Men dreaming of men: Using Mitch Walker's "double animus" in pastoral care. *The Harvard Theological Review, 86*(2), 219-232.

DeAngelo, David. (2005). *Double your dating: What every man should know about how to be successful with women.* Self-published.

Deida, David. (2004). *The way of the superior man: A spiritual guide to mastering the challenges of women, work and sexual desire* (2nd ed.). Boulder, CO: Sounds True.

Deleuze, Gilles, & Guattari, Félix. (1987). *A thousand plateaus: Capitalism and schizophrenia* (B. Massumi, Trans.). Minneapolis: University of Minnesota Press.

Ehrenreich, Barbara. (2009). *Bright-sided: How the relentless promotion of positive thinking has undermined America.* New York: Metropolitan Books.

Fox, Matthew. (2008). *The hidden spirituality of men: Ten metaphors to awaken the sacred masculine.* Novato, CA: New World Library.

Gelfer, Joseph. (2009). *Numen, old men: Contemporary masculinities and the problem of patriarchy.* London: Equinox Publishing.

Gelfer, Joseph. (2003). *The little book of student bollocks.* Chichester: Summersdale Publishers.

Gelfer, Joseph. (2002). *The little book of office bollocks.* Chichester: Summersdale Publishers.

Gelfer, Joseph. (2002). *The little book of toilet graffiti.* Chichester: Summersdale Publishers.

Gilligan, Carol. (1993). *In a different voice: Psychological theory and women's development* (2nd ed.). Cambridge, MA: Harvard University Press.

Gingold, Alfred. (1991). *Fire in the john.* New York: St Martin's Press.

Gray, John. (1992). *Men are from mars, women are from Venus: A practical guide for improving communication and getting what you want in relationships.* New York: HarperCollins.

Hampson, Sally. (2008). Looking to God for relationship advice. *The Global and Mail.* Retrieved from http://www.theglobeandmail.com/life/article665448.ece

Harris, I. M. (1997). Ten tenets of male spirituality. *The Journal of Men's Studies,* 6(1), 29-53.

Hartley, Leslie Poles. (1953). *The Go-Between.* London: Hamish Hamilton.

Hayes, Shannon. (2010). *Radical homemakers: Reclaiming domesticity from a consumer culture.* Richmondville, NY: Left to Write Press.

James, Stephen and David Thomas. (2009). *Wild things: The art of nurturing boys.* Carol Stream, IL: Tyndale House Publishers.

Johnson, Rick. (2006). *Better dads, stronger sons: How fathers can guide boys to become men of character.* Grand Rapids, MI: Revell.

Johnson, Toby. (2000). *Gay spirituality: The role of gay identity in the transformation of human consciousness.* Los Angeles: Alyson Books.

Jung, Carl. (2009). *The red book* (S. Shamdasani, ed.). New York: W. W. Norton.

The Masculinity Conspiracy

Kinsey, Alfred. (1998). *Sexual behavior in the human male.* Bloomington, IN: University of Indiana Press.

Kipnis, Aaron. (1992). The blessing of the green man. In C. Harding (Ed.), *Wingspan: Inside the men's movement* (pp. 161-165). New York: St Martin's Press.

Lawlor, Robert. (1989). *Earth honoring: The new male sexuality.* Rochester, VT: Inner Traditions.

Mansfield, Harvey. (2006). *Manliness.* New Haven, CT: Yale University Press.

Mazis, Glen. (1993). *The trickster, magician & grieving man: Reconnecting men with earth.* Santa Fe, NM: Bear & Co.

Moore, Henrietta. (1988). *Feminism and anthropology.* Minneapolis: University of Minnesota Press.

Moore, Robert, & Gillette, Douglas. (1990). *King, warrior, magician, lover: Rediscovering the archetypes of the mature masculine.* New York: HarperCollins.

Rolls, Mitchell. (2000). Robert Lawlor tells a "white" lie. *Journal of Australian Studies*, 66: 211-218; 284-286.

Rosaldo, Michelle. (1974). Woman, culture, and society: A theoretical overview. In M. Z. Rosaldo & L. Lamphere (Eds.), *Woman, culture, and society* (pp. 17-42). Stanford, CA: Stanford University Press.

Rutter, Peter. (1990). *Sex in the forbidden zone: When men in power—therapists, doctors, clergy, teachers, and others—betray women's trust.* London: Mandala.

Sapolsky, Robert. (2006). A natural history of peace. *Foreign Affairs*, 85(1): 104-120.

Shakespeare, Nicholas. (2000). *Bruce Chatwin: A biography*. New York: Doubleday.

Stoletenberg, John. (1989). *Refusing to be a man: Essays on sex and justice*. Portland, OR: Breitenbush Books.

Stemmeler, M. L. (1996). Empowerment: The construction of gay religious identity. In B. Krondorfer (Ed.), *Men's bodies, men's gods: Male identities in a (post-) Christian culture* (pp. 94-107). New York: New York University Press.

Tacey, David. (1997). *Remaking men: Jung, spirituality and social change*. London: Routledge.

Wall, John. (2010). *Ethics in light of childhood*. Washington, DC: Georgetown University Press.

Wilber, Ken. (2000). *Sex, ecology, spirituality: The spirit of evolution* (2nd ed.). Boston: Shambhala.

Wink, Walter. (1992). *Engaging the powers: Discernment and resistance in a world of domination*. Minneapolis: Fortress Press.

Yalom, Irvine. (1980). *Existential psychotherapy*. New York: Basic Books.

Zipes, Jack. (1992). Spreading myths about fairy tales: A critical commentary on Robert Bly's Iron John. *New German Critique, 55*(Winter), 3-19.

ABOUT THE AUTHOR

Joseph Gelfer is author of *Numen, Old Men: Contemporary Masculine Spiritualities and the Problem of Patriarchy* (Equinox Publishing, 2009) and editor of *2012: Decoding the Countercultural Apocalypse* (Equinox Publishing, 2011). He is also editor of *Journal of Men, Masculinities and Spirituality*, an open access journal available at www.jmmsweb.org, and *The Best of Journal of Men, Masculinities and Spirituality* (Gorgias Press, 2010).

For further information visit his website at www.gelfer.net.

www.ingramcontent.com/pod-product-compliance
Lightning Source LLC
Chambersburg PA
CBHW060311290526
45789CB00001B/485